ARK

EDITED BY

PETER O'LEARY

*

FLOOD EDITIONS

CHICAGO

ARK

RONALD JOHNSON

Published by Flood Editions
www.floodeditions.com
Paperback ISBN 979-8-9857874-7-4
Design and composition by Crisis
Printed in Canada on acid-free, recycled paper
This book was made possible in part through
a grant from the Poetry Foundation

The editor would like to thank Elspeth Healey, Special Collections librarian
at the Kenneth Spencer Research Library, for her help in locating images
reproduced in this edition, courtesy of Special Collections. Likewise, he
would like to thank Jeni Crone for her help in preparing the manuscript.

Second paperback edition, 2025

A NOTE ON THE TEXT

This edition is based on the complete *ARK* published by Living Batch Press in 1996. The text has been checked for accuracy against typescripts and previous publications of the poem. Some corrections have been made accordingly, with several missing lines restored.

Previous editions of the poem vary the leading to reflect single- and double-spacing in Johnson's typescript. However, for greater legibility, this edition adopts a basic leading that is uniform.

PETER O'LEARY

THE FOUNDATIONS

1–33

"The universe is a slumbering animal
that has visions" —Edward Dahlberg

"anything shut in with you
can sing" —Gertrude Stein

BEAM 1

Over the rim
body of earth   rays exit sun
rest to full velocity to eastward pinwheeled in a sparrow's

eye
—Jupiter compressed west to the other—

wake waves on wave in wave striped White Throat song

along the reversal of one

contra-

centrifugal

water to touch, all knowledge

as if a several silver

backlit in gust.

All night the golden fruit fell softly to the air,

pips ablaze, our eyes skinned back.

Clouds loom below. Pocked moon fills half the sky. Stars

comb out its lumen

horizon

in a gone-to-seed dandelion

as of snowflakes hitting black water, time, and again,

then dot the plain

186,282 cooped-up angels tall as appletrees

caryatid

one sudden tide of day

O

wide bloom the pathed earth yawn

on purpose porpoised pattern

this reeled world whistling joist its polished fields of sun

pulse race in a vase of beings, bearings

all root fold forms upon

to center eternity

or enter it

instruments of change.

and bareback as Pegasus guess us

BEAM 2

Cloud to ground, the ice electrons move—negative to positive—in stepped bright thrust. Each fifty-yard step occurs in less than one one-millionth of a second, the whole zigzag one to ten yards in luminous diameter. This but corona to a rose-prickle core hotter than the surface of the sun. Positive to negative—the stroke returns gigantic spark, its many-stroked flash a flicker faster than the eye. Every "point" on this returned jagged channel knocks molecules for miles in links . . .

The circumambient!

in balanced dissent:
enlightenment—on abysm bent.

Angels caged

in what I see,
externity in gauged
antiphony.

A lineaged clarity.

7

(Mid-age. Brought to my knee.)

1935–70

The altitude

unglued

A god in a cloud,

aloud.

Exactitude the flood.

BEAM 3

I KNEW THEN THAT I HAD COME TO A PLACE
—one after another (pale sulphur yellow, pale golden citron)
as a radius of moths, bull's-eye to light—

months dandelion to the instant

"cornea": The horny transparent membrane
in the forepart of the eye
through which the rays of light pass.

"corona": A halo or luminous circle—crown—around
one of the heavenly bodies.
A spectre seen during total eclipse of suns
or circumference
of a radiated composite flower.

mind over (under, behind, ahead) matter
fireearthair & water
imagining themselves cornflowers
as seen by man

/ of the shuffle, flux to core, the last card turned the first /

"The Juggler"

shape-shifter/mirror of forms/the ever-

uncoiling, slip-slap quicksilver

A WALKING STREAM

THE WAKING DREAM

"At the same time I saw myself in him, reflected as in a mirror, and it seemed to me that I was looking at myself through his eyes. But another feeling told me there was nothing in front of me but the blue sky and that within myself a window opened . . ."

through which The Voices called each to each

:   How to explain   :

the blind design,

or make it sane behind its shine?

How to inquire

within

the fire?

through which reached hand to write

where the inner regions, tangled along polarized

garland, turn faster than the outer

BEAM 4

The human eye, a sphere of waters and tissue, absorbs an energy that has come ninety-three million miles from another sphere, the sun. The eye may be said to be sun in other form.

It is part of a spectrum of receptors, and if we could only "see" more widely the night sky would be "brighter" than the moon. Matter smaller than the shortest wavelength of light cannot be seen.

Pressure on the surface of an eye makes vision, though what these same pressures focus to the radial inwardness of a dragonfly in flight is unimaginable. Through pressure also, the head-over-heels is crossed right-side-up, in eye as camera. (It is possible to take a cow's eyeball and thin the rear wall of it with a knife, fit it front forward in a tube, and the tube pointed at an elm will image an upside-down elm.)

The front of the eye is a convex glass, alive, and light bent through its curve strikes a lens. This lens is behind an iris—pushing it into the shape of a volcano. In light, the iris appears as a rayed core of color, its center hole dilating dark to day, transformed instantly into what man's twinned inner hemispheres call sight.

The retina is its bowl-shaped back—the cones at retinal center growing through intersections with rods, toward rods at the rim. Through this mesh, ray seizes ray to see. In the rods there is a two-part molecule that is unlinked by light. One quantum of light unlinks one molecule, and five rods are needed to perceive the difference. Some stars are at this threshold, and can only be seen by the sides of the eyes. The eye can see a wire .01 inch in diameter at a distance of 100 yards. The retina itself seeks equilibrium.

Though to look at the sun directly causes blindness, sight is an intricately precise tip of branched energy that has made it possible to measure the charge of solar storm, or to calculate nova. It is possible that all universe is of a similar form.

Our eyes are blue for the same reason sky is, a scattering of reflectors: human eyes have only brown pigment.

In the embryo two stalks push from the brain, through a series of infoldings, to form optic cups. Where the optic cup reaches surface, the surface turns in and proliferates in the shape of an ingrowing mushroom. The last nerve cells to form are those farthest from light.

If I sit at my table and look at the shaft of light which enters a glass filled with water—and exits rainbow—then move my head to the left, the shaft and glass move right, and the window behind them, left. If I stand up and step to the table, the glass at its edge moves downward, while the far end of the table, and the window with it, rise straight up in the air.

No one knows the first man to stare long at a waterfall, then shift his gaze to the cliff face at its side, to find the rocks at once flow upward. But we have always known the eye to be unsleeping, and that all men are lidless Visionaries through the night. Mind & Eye are a logarithmic spiral coiled from periphery. This is called a "spiral sweep"—a biological form which combines (as do galaxies) economy with beauty. (We define "beauty" from symmetrical perceptions: *subjects observing a flickered pulsation of light have seen something like a Catherine wheel reversing rotation, with a center of fine detail*). Men have found cells sensitive to light in the hearts of snails.

The human lens grows flatter for looking across a prairie, and the sparrow is able to see the seed beneath its bill—and in the same instant the hawk descending. A cat watches the sparrow-at-the-end-of-the-world in a furred luminosity of infra-reds, enormous purples.

After a long time of light, there began to be eyes, and light began looking with itself. At the exact moment of death the pupils open full width.

BEAM 5, THE VOICES

the loom, the x of the instant
looped to time: windmill-ply of the plenum, laced
ion

eon
:the actuals, like kingfishers
flashing across pools: minnow beneath flicker:
image to image:
that-which-consumes and
—blaze within blaze within blaze—

that-which-gives-light:
"the quick, the ag-ile, Ag-nis, ig-nis"
center/circumference in

one

:the outside in a nutshell:

our magnifying
being

:

```
       c i r c
       l e c i
       r c l e


          o
       m o o n


      i n m i n d i n


      ɑ e  ɑ e  ɑ e  ɑ e  ɑ e
    w  v  w  v  w  v  w  v  w  v


       eyeyeye


          .



form from form from form from form

"play'd by the picture of No-body"

whose *bright stripes & broad stars*

pinpointeddyshuttlecrossroadssword

(a-hinged-magnetic-up-and-down-on)

all a bowed honeycomb space become
```

Music, anatomy—an atomed Euridice

as if of fireflies in relief

to turning earth

&

thunder, cymbal mazed in timpani of smattering,

arm's electron's long way

back

radius at which the shock wave relaxes

(30° above and below

bisect spark)

*

AND THEN THE THREEFOLD TREEFIRE STROKE-IN-STROKE

AGAIN

—obliquity to the ecliptic—

"bear" (Polar) among the asphodel, singing Bach's Unaccompanied

Cello.

Ear (solar) in Bosch of metanoias—nose to nose Is, Is, Is

(noise)

Polyphony of epiphanies.

BEAM 6, THE MUSICS

Let flick his tail, the darkling Lion, down to the primal huddle fiddling
DNA.

Let the Elephant ruffle the elements in The Great Looped Nebula with
his uplift trunk.

Let the Binary, orange, emerald, and blue, in the foot of Andromeda
run awhisker with Mouse.

Let the Dickcissel, in Cock's-foot, Foxtail, & Tottering, ring one molec-
ular ornamentation on Tau Ceti.

Let the Switch Snake lilt bluegrass back and forth between pellucid
cells.

Let Porcupine rattle quill, in a Cassiopeia of Hollyhock.

Let the whinny of Pigeons' wings trigger similar strains from elm to Tri-
angulum.

Let a score for matter's staccato to cornstalk be touted to stars clus-
tering The Archer's wrist.

Let the stripes of Zebra be in time with the imaginary House of
Mozart, on Jupiter.

Sound is sea: pattern lapping pattern. If we erased the air and slowed the sound of a struck tuning fork in it, it would make two sets of waves interlocking the invisibility in opposite directions.

As the prong of the fork moves one way, it compresses the air at its front, which layer in turn relieves its compression by expanding the layer in front, and so back to back. As it starts the other direction it leaves the air in front (opposite) immediately rarefied. The air beyond this expands to the rarefaction—itself becoming rarefied—forth and forth.

Compression rarefaction compression rarefaction: these alternate equidistant forces travel at the rate of 1,180 feet per second through the elasticity of air, four times that through water (whale to singing whale), and fifteen times as fast through pure steel. Men have put ear to earth to hear in advance of air.

Pattern laps pattern, and as they joined, Charles Ives heard the nineteenth century in one ear, and the twentieth out the other, then commenced to make a single music of them. The final chord of the Second

Symphony is a reveille of all notes at once, his Fourth of July ends with a fireworks of thirteen rhythmic patterns zigzagging through the winds and brasses, seven percussion lines crisscrossing these, the strings divided in twenty-fours going up and down every which way —and all in FFFF.

Both tuning fork and Fourth are heard by perturbations of molecules, through ever more subtle stumbling blocks, in spiral ricochet, to charged branches treeing a brain.

The outer earshell leads to a membrane drum—and what pressure needed to sound this drum is equal to the intensity of light and heat received from a fifty-watt electric bulb at the distance of three thousand miles in empty space. (Though sound cannot travel, as light, through the void.) At the threshold of hearing the eardrum may be displaced as little as a diameter of the smallest atom, hydrogen.

This starts a "hammer" to strike an "anvil" which nudges a "stirrup"— all, bones—against a drum known as The Oval Window. Shut to air, this window vibrates another windowed membrane, tuning a compressed fluid between. *Here, also, is couched our sense of the vertical.*

A resonance is set up in a spiral shell-shaped receptor tuned with yet another, also spiral, membrane. This is the pith of labyrinth, and as sound waves themselves it trembles two directions at once, crosswise and lengthwise.

The mind begins early to select from the buzz and humdrum, till most men end hearing nothing, when the earth speaks, but their own voices. Henry David Thoreau seems to have been the first man to re-learn to hear that *Moto Perpetuo* of the actual: the Greeks strung their lyre to the planets, but Thoreau heard his stretched from first dark sparrow to last dog baying moon.

While a bat uses its ears to see, its optics overtones, the fly hears only in frequencies of its own (and other) flywings. I know the housefinch singing outside the window just now heard its own song with slower and lower ear than mine, but I do not know what this means, or how it rings in finchskull. (Though all animals have an auditory range that includes hearing what they can eat, and what can eat them.)

A man once set out to see birds, but found instead he'd learned to listen: an ear better unwinds the simultaneous warblers in a summer birchwood. There, he came upon an Orpheus, all marble, holding a spiral shell to the ear of his Euridice. Turning the other way, he saw Orpheus again, listening to harmonics of midges in sun, the meadow like a nightingale around him. Cat's purr, moth-wing.

The physicists tell us that all sounding bodies are in a state of stationary vibration, and that when the word *syzygy* last shook atoms, its boundary was an ever slighter pulse of heat, and hesitation of heat. Matter delights in music, and became Bach. Its dreams are the abyss and empyrean, and to that end, may move, in time, the stones themselves to sing.

BEAM 8

Line eye us.

Web stir us.

—as the eye leaves outside of itself the object it sees—

the mind weaves it

of itself

incessant shuttle to external's

shelf

point . circle . point

(a double cone in counterpoint)

within, without

AS I PASS THROUGH A WINDOW REFLECTED BEHIND ME

in a glass

held in my hand, behold:

wind Os wind Os

wind Os wind Os

wind Os wind Os

wind Os wind Os

—ripple-intersecting circles
Open, Close—

in equipoise through the nuclei's "quadrupole
moments"

mag-nets-nets-nets

&c.

... beyond utterance.

Linkings, inklings,
around the stem & branches of the nervetree—
shudder and shutterings, sensings.

SENSE *sings.*
"A world where chaos and cosmos are interlaced and superim-
posed,
where anything may happen,

but nothing happens twice"

—perceive! perceive! Reality is "make" believe.

(that everything happens at once is the form of The Dance)

:THAT EAR IS FIRMAMENT TO CRICKET
THUMBPRINT FLOOR TO GALAXY:

I am alive as long as there is fire in my head

and sing for my supper, out of the mouth of the dead.

( )

Ernst Mach

hallucinated a candle

lit

in a beaker of water:

hallucinated

means

"to mind travel"

(or, the language torques focus as black holes of space

are pores to a skin of a face we're in)

What *it* is looking at is the Aught ignite, each bud

a lamp,

bent in water beaker

behind your eyes curved

on reflecting surface of cylinder

(with triple cross-barred window behind head mirrored four sails

to soapbubble

polyverse)

—*only matter could "make up" anti-matter*—

The Definition of

Perception:

)(

(like seeing gravity throwing apples

sideways off trees)

within

"*Conical refraction;* the refraction of a single ray of light, under certain conditions, into an infinite number of rays in the form of a hollow, luminous cone, and consisting of two kinds, namely, *external conical refraction* and *internal conical refraction*, the ray in the former issuing from the refraction crystal as a cone with its vertex at the point of emergence, and in the latter being converted into a cone on entering the crystal, and issuing

cylinder."

(the glass on Webster)

from the roots "break" "branch"

as the leaves part on Leonardo's Orpheus of Proportions
in flight among the square, circle
square, circle square of

BEAM 9

Daedal, the seamless seen——the screen of seem:

Lave & Weave

Wave & Leave

le dur désir de durer

(sound as clear as light, for smithy)

-node-to-gyre-

"And then went down to the"

planet

at about the velocity of a leaf drift

down from oak a windless day, and landed pink sky stippled

apricock, upon a terra-cotta sand.

to transmit *sic transit*

in excelsis

this

BEAM 10

daimon diamond Monad I
Adam Kadmon in the sky

BEAM 11, FINIAL

The thrust

is thirst:

enough to whirl Neptune, in its orbit, three billion miles

away

or curl the fern stalk up.

Coalescent holocaust

(which means The-Whole-Growing-Together-through-Fire)

to gyroscope

emits in layers rays of many lengths.

Its corona is the moth-

winged shape

a float of dust on water makes

from out an apple

transfixed upon a knitting needle

spun half submerged.

It is said the sun blinds us because it is a HOLE

in the three-dimensional scenery.

—and light "diminishes in inverse proportion to the square

of the distance"

but the imaginary sphere

it illuminates, increases in the same

proportion—

Its Zodiacal Light is in the form of a lens

the lash of which intersects earth.

It is one-ten-thousandth the diameter of its "system"

as is ovum to human.

VISION is seeing as the sun sees.

"midway between the absolute

and man"

(Fludd said)

The Mind & Eye, the solar system, galaxy

are spirals coiled from periphery

—i.e. Catherine wheels—

of their worlds.

Whorls.

PARTICULAR SOLAR PLEXUS, COMPRESSER,

COMPLEXER:

plus ringed by minus

quickened in interlocking octaves

into a daffodil

(intricately fluted)

atop a hill

upon an ochre, blue, and white swirled world below

How to inquire

within the fire?

What thinnest spoke-infolded core

of farthest star

invoke, in what we are?

Were?

Rodin did

he said

("each thing is merely the limit of the flame

to which it owes its existence")

CONFLUXUS RADIORUM

BEAM 12

⊙ is the symbol for Sun, the circumference brought to focus at a point. Its outward manifestation is life, just as mind itself seems to unfold some answering chrysanthemum. Beneath a maze pattern on a wall of the church of St. Savino, in Piacenza, the inscription reads: THIS LABYRINTH REVEALS THE STRUCTURE OF THE WORLD. Convoluted of sun and dust, shut dark in a skull, the labyrinth is its own clue. Our lot is puzzlement.

Right auricle, right ventricle, lungs: left auricle, left ventricle, aorta: aorta means "to lift" or "heave" and is the great trunk of perception. Branches, from the top of its arch, network the light in our heads— out of a stuff of rays, particles, and pulses: the artificer of reality.

If we represent the three-dimensional world we live in as a line, ray, or passage, between the fourth dimension as a globe, then as the universe expands this line describes involutions within that globe. This is the brain of time.

What footprint is left in the snow of flesh by an event? Thinking about thinking moves atoms—however mirrored: and so, as in a rainbow the architecture of light is revealed, mind is a revelation of matter. These wrinkled lobes of flesh, in fact, are more sensitive than the surface of water, and some have watched small eyelids tremble in the womb and wondered could a molecule remember.

The first anatomists likened the brain, pulp and rind, to an orange. Its beginnings are a mulberry of cells, and all desire and despair are seeded in its un- and in-foldings.

Both consciousness and the unconscious "collect." It is as if some eons-old mind (in a time when it could do those things) cast the future on its cold eye, saw Plato's cave, and became our brains. Where it will look with us—through "cavernous Earth / Of labyrinthine intricacy, twenty-seven folds of opakeness"—is what you and I are doing this instant. Still, beneath the frontal lobes, at the stem of consciousness, is that reptilian speechless gaze. Man is amphibian to oblivion.

From the ape at my shoulderblade I see angels. Our embryo dreamt the fishes' sleep, became a ripple, leap-frogged itself, and later a mammal: perception is a slingshot drawn back to first plasm.

BEAM 13

CHRYSOS
anthemon

f lux f lux f lux f
lux f lux f lux f l
ux f lux f lux f lu
x f lux f lux f lux
f lux f lux f lux f

BEAM 14

Eden, glossolalia of light

Mountain the gods stept from, spoke to fork

some sparkling *logos*

as *O hoher Baum im Ohr!*

quadricornutus serpens, caduceus phantastikon, or

la ou nos la voions plus espesse

vas, at the same time orb and eggshaped

O

Matrix of Harmonies

orders, opening back, beyond, and within, Laocoön of cocoon

splint crystal, *glaux,* gray matter spun

"Out of thy head I sprung"

thread not a dream by a single Being, but one of *omni-*

silk-seed of waves hummed back

vast cortex

tensile, unstill

He who "would chain fire,

and have the wind move in regiments

of cubed air"

(As Bohm posited: at zeropoint

of energy

a cubic centimeter of space = 10,000,000,000 tons

uranium) underneathunder

unutterable number

an intricate quiet

centripetal

FIAT

he who

obsessed by light,

possessed by sight:

cellophane in cellophane of salamander slid within a flame

(to pin to the shimmer a name)

Beauty is easy.

It is the Beast that is the secret.

A COERCED SPLENDOR!

"it escapes from its sphere

as from a hole"

mil-

lion-hued

—its symmetries like trees with long shadows

—

A mirror held

to the horror

"we can imagine a butterfly

to pass back into the chrysalis"

like a cat's eye in

time.

at the end of its tether

the inter-

stellar

BEAM 15, CORNERSTONE

Thoreau: *"How can that depth be fathomed where a man may see himself reflected? The rill I stopped to drink at I drink in more than I expected. I satisfy and still provoke the thirst of thirsts. I do not drink in vain. I mark that brook as if I had swallowed a water snake that would live in my stomach. I have swallowed something worth the while. The day is not what it was before I stopped to drink. Ah, I shall hear from that draught! It is not in vain that I have drunk. I have drunk an arrowhead. It flows from where all fountains rise. How many ova have I swallowed? Who knows what will be hatched within me? There were some seeds of thought, methinks, floating in that water, which are expanding in me. The man must not drink of the running streams, the living waters, who is not prepared to have all nature reborn in him—to suckle monsters. The snake in my stomach lifts his head to my mouth at the sound of running water. When was it that I swallowed a snake? I have got rid of the snake in my stomach. I drank of stagnant waters once. That accounts for it. I caught him by the throat and drew him out, and had a well day after all. Is there not such a thing as getting rid of the snake which you have swallowed when young, when thoughtless you stooped and drank at stagnant waters, which has worried you in your waking hours and in your sleep ever since, and appropriated the life that was yours? Will he not*

ascend into your mouth at the sound of running water? Then catch him

boldly by the head and draw him out, though you may think his tail be

curled about your vitals ————————————————————

BEAM 16, THE VOICES

plumb line

"For Orpheus' lute was strung with poets' sinews"
CROSS*SECTION OF KANSAS LILAC I SAT IN AT

11

:nodal mosaic of rays slant streetlight

Pole Star naillike at canopy:

:moon behind cloud beyond bloom within its own dark afterimage

axial twig, live silver:

:a tranquility of minute balances tremolo near leaf tip

fireflies (magnified 1,000 times):

:the sound of a great black cloth ripping apart

WHERE THE DEITY DWELLS

THE APE IS TO APPEAR

as "*the shadow dogs the body*

of one who walks in the sun"

(hidden Euridice, whose face is ice)

MAKE MUSIC!

Socrates' three dreams

said.

HYMN HELIOS

out error's scatter sight's spectrum pattern

"limn electric"

IN THE AIRE

(Heraclitus on the sistrum)

perception is physics' intrinsic Its knit

&

/

or

Mr. Curious Hermes

(as the Greeks had season's quarters counterspiral

by entwined instinct image:

Mage)

twin snakes wrapt round our vitals

out plinth of time

"piVot"

—winged—

"crescent on circle from cross"

(or metamorphosis-outshines-beast-round Homo

Maximus,

us

)

:ACT ICARUS EACH CREVICE:

Mr. Curious

said

—why we cannot, so close it is the sun,

see Intellect—

... *Though weave's riddle angles Angells bee* ...

butterfly-net senses' instant's

limits,

quantum's

sums

ABRAXAS IS EXACT OF FACT

"as if"

(by magic)

trans-ex-spiring what we call time

presence

behind an appearance

"the backparts

of"

BEAM 17, THE BOOK OF ORPHEUS

FOR ROBERT DUNCAN

That the story is plied in threes, and is thus a parable of SPACE.

First Orpheus plucks a music upon the Shell of earth, a form from
which some say the intervals between strings are those the planets
resonate. This is the body of man, where lion lie with lamb in The
Imaginary Menagerie, where tree waltz rock down to the rainbow
angle at interacting atoms.

That music is the art of TIME. Its work is Abstract and Mathematick,
but is created in our own image. That the orders of lyre and year
have such a close fit one could not slip a grassblade between.

Next, that he crosses the threshold of the unconscious to find Euridice
by that same power, but must lose her at brink by looking back,
mirror-warp to waking.

Last, this first "maker" was torn apart by irrational women (for, it is
said, preaching the love of man for man) so he is only a head now
bearing down Being, only a singing. The lyre-head then washes
seaflash to some inner cave of prophecy till the sun itself (its father)
hush it to the faintest rustling from a run of stars.

That wonder takes all forms—Euridice, slip-knot through flesh, abreast
the well of light, hand dipped in mercury through breath of earth
—and thus is One Form.

That he who, fireshook head to foot, mistake the sun to speak, shall
see the world from scratch. Wobble to pole: Great Balls of Fire,
exquisite sediment.

FIRST DREAM

There is no wall
to it all.
Up, goes the widening ball,
till I fall.

SECOND DREAM

(thunder) I sprint as music up a hill,
spirit in the grip of unison, as if Scarlatti'd
meadowlarked particles.
At top I find a woman carved of wood, who in my arms
turns carefully yellow daffodils.

A figurehead Euridice
is what I hold.

He who has seized one pebble shall climb a mountain.

He who has understood the wit of birds will split the weight of wings.

That Angels are not subject to gravity, and are therefore a cuckleburr of senses, apples all eyes and hearing spheres.

That one prism holds the spectrumed "glory" as surely as whole populations of droplets strummed by sun.

That the action of the universe is metamorphosis—its articulation, metaphor. White crow, black swan, these are the hinges of Heaven.

A MEMORABLE FANCY

As I was walking in my Garden, an Angel in an apple tree saw me, and spoke: *I drink the air before me* momentum a beam lighttouch-stonearc seen after rain ray bright sequence innermost outermost band outermost innermost Aristotle thus explained the circular scattered incident magnified drop filled with internal reflections refract of constants at obliquely index two all directions quivalent significant axispassing zero tangent surface transmitted again split passages not ordinarily visible of angle illuminated at all impact simultaneously infinitely the vicinity backscattered toward sun through the center three grazes in its original directions so do they bend back toward the forward univaries most slowly with changes in other words gather together regions of imaginary intensity in a sky filled with real waves.

That clockwise, counterclockwise, as blue bindweed to honeysuckle, the cosmos is an organism spirally closed on itself, into the pull of existence. In the beginning there was the Word—for each man, magnetized by onrush, is Adam to his Tyger.

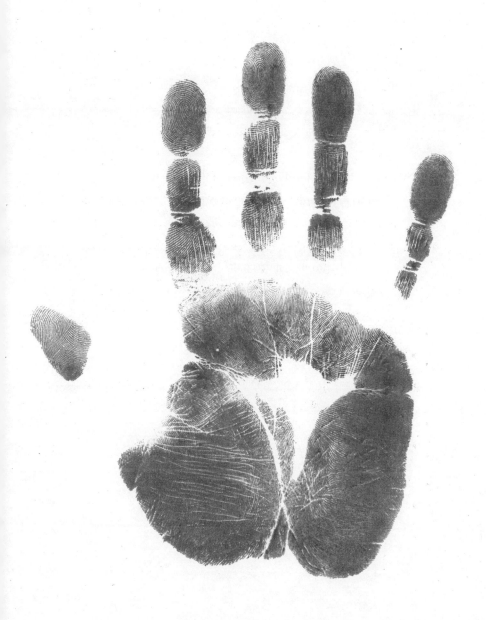

BEAM 18

BEAM 19

lilac, winedark

sun-gold in chopped scarlet

starred

equilateral equangular quinquangles

(like to those balls stitched twelve patchwork of color)

skiey Okeanos

clouds like loud chords

—whose contours their contours pun—

out of a drop of water-that-does-not-wet-the-hand

become a blue mirrored ball on emerald lawn

(with dandelions for

miles)

BEAM 20, LABYRINTHUS

FOR EURIDICE

It is lucid as Euclid. It is a splay of space and planes overlapping and interpenetrating from the stairs rising in all directions. Pasted on water, it is separated by folding screens concealing everything in the picture. It is as if you yourself were your own onlooker. Simultaneously from all sides, bird's-eye view it settles within its metallic sheen, framed by bright lines. It is a mirage of parachutes brought together and separated by forces of five separate foregrounds opening like Chinese boxes. Small windows open and shut in a photograph of the earth from the moon hung on the walls of an imaginary Musée de l'Homme, where it plays its own elastic lace of shadows. Stroboscopic radiolaria divespin slow motion from its apparent perimeter, penumbra of wind tossed willow round rose halo. It's not that we're getting slower, it's that the world is going faster. One above another, in globes of clarity and camouflage, between it appear mutually irreconcilable realities. Backward in double exposures odds and ends veined with gnarls and bird's eyes simulate collisions with it. It rises and falls through the repercussions of songs of birds, as through a lake, connected by a central axis suddenly reversing in depth so that what was the back face now is the front one, and so forth.

O

Tree

into the World,

Man

the chosen

˙Rose out of Chaos:

Song

Thunder amid held daffodil,

the hills of yellow celandine in sudden sun

electrum

"when the light walks."

When the light walks, clockwise, counterclockwise,

atoms memorize the firefly's wing

silhouette twenty-foot elm leaf

(worm's-eye view through three crisscross timothy stalks).

A blue hinged green at edge, the twilight

sinks as if half swimmer

—ankles in wrinkle through wood turtle

swallowing scarlet strawberry,

waist deep the warp then roof of star split clover, one pale

eye spool rayed Orion

thistle silk through soil particle—

to Euridice. Head deep

in neither ·

aether, nether:

"You will find, to the left of The House of *Hades*, a spring . . .

one white-leafed cypress at its side."

"Sometimes the prophet sees the image of Glory

in the midst of a cloud;

but the angel-messenger is invisible

because the angelic fire is too pure for one to see.

When one sees the fire flaming

up from the distance

one is only seeing the smoke that

surrounds it.

Moreover the angel asks:

What do you see?"

"I have seen the Eternal

interior,

not ocular, vision"

reply.

PALMS

B_e

the man that walk in the way of day and night

like a tree of water, leaf

chaff which the wind

stand in

imagine the earth set against sun,

uttermost parts like a potter's O: trembling sands round about

Arise, and ray.

Stand in

your own heart,

and be still.

the light upon us

in time to the voice of ice:

no throat out in the multitude of ions belled But shout

for joy.

O

save me for

the grave who

all the night make I my bed to swim

·

O

lion, compass

turn

to an end but arrows sing

Out of the mouth of

moon and the stars,

What is man, that made him angels, beasts

to a perpetual end: the gates in the gates of net hid

snared in the turn into sight.

:let them be

imagined.

moved in the secret

ear to hear:

bird to mountain eyelid cup.

They speak tongue tried in a furnace of earth,

on every side,

I sleep the *sleep* of

all, not

one.

The lines are fallen to me

in the night seasons.

as the apple of the eye under the shadow of wings,

lion in secret likeness.

voice

shot out lightnings of many waters.

candle:

my steps under me,

consumed.

rose dust before the wind

rock above those that rise up

:man

edge to the world.

sun circuit it: eye in honeycomb heart, hand. name for

ever ever moved

in time the fire shall seed imagined form.

worm shake the womb: I am poured out like water

into the dust of death.

closed unicorn

the ends of the world shall turn

green shadow run.

earth flood into the head

gates; doors; gates; doors; all day enlarged:

an even lace in light and flesh,

the voice of

waters

upon many waters,

The voice of flame shake wild voice from the grave:

down to the remembranch of morning. moved mountain to stand

in my blood, dust dancing:

and ear rock rock out of the spirit hand

out of my mind:

I have heard

My times

lips put to silence; a pavilion of tongues.

cut off from eyes: bones roaring all the day long summer.

in a time when place compass song

I harp an earth full of breath: the sea stood fast.

their works

magnify the exalt together.

matter open wide

clouds like great mountains the fountain of

light shall we see light.

grass-sword heart, time: not again the

seed tree my flesh

before love,

not continually

beauty to consume like a moth: but of the clay,

ears opened from great congregation.

whisper lift

from everlasting to everlasting

meat in praise,

within me: deep call to

deep harp

out arm, and the light

scattered with the forgotten

face,

matter: writer.

though the earth be removed,

There is

a river, not moved:

were moved: in the fire.

with the sound of a trumpet wind ends of the round

ear to a parable:

I will open my dark

upon the harp

of compass

inward like the beasts shined before me.

I fold a thousand hills.

I would blood the most High:

frame silence as

self

set in order.

the inward parts: and in the hidden snow walls

the land of a green child is

gone back:

the altogether become one

ion!

the trembling over, a dove at rest

in tempest

:Day and night the midst of it.

thereof: magnify hid changes, words sword the swallow

from falling, light

the shadow lion set on fire, arrow an earth.

I will sing and

Awake my salt to the clouds.

speak to the voice of the great snail sun whirlwind blood

from the run return and go round scatter

the ends of the earth

return up and down.

I will sing

aloud in the morning: to tremble the breaches

of astonishment.

I shall be moved as a bowing wall

delight

in the balance,

every man to his marrow

bend in secret at the perfect fall all flesh come.

waves, and the tumult in uttermost token:

morning and evening

river the year on every side

Make

a joyful noise

through the flood on foot:

moved as silver net over our heads went fire-shine smoke, Sing

shook snow from the fountain of clouds.

I sink

stranger to prayer

out of the deep waters.

flow me, face to my soul, in my thirst

let it become

love turned backward love magnified: wonder lay wait

in the little hills, long moon, mown grass

showers in the dust gold corn

city of the sun all shall call a dream

ignorant heart: I have put my trust in smoke.

axes upon axes cast fire
in the land.
signs: the borders of turtledove-dissolve: east, west,
full of mixture
ring out, the mountains of sleep.
waking:
The water saw:
The skies sent out a sound:

thunder path the great know utter our fathers told
us divided
cloud, and all the night with light of
kindled doors
rained down as sand,
the years a wind in hand, locust,
sycamore frost.

the hail flocks to angels fire consumed blood
like water pointed to shine

Turn us again, O
to take deep root, filled with the shadow sent boughs out sea,
branch to the river.
hedge wood and the wild field look down
hand planted with fire,

Turn us again, O

noise to palm, harp psaltery.

Blow the secret place of thunder: wheat

foundations of silence not still, joined like a wheel;

stubble before wind.

flameflesh the sparrow nest through; the rain spring out of earth;

voice answer me.

O turn unto her: instrument

I cannot come forth.

The north and the south

in vision alter the thing for ever,

void edge down to the ground how short time is:

What man shall not see death?

footsteps the years past, a sleep: consumed by number

we have seen beauty in the secret place

shadowings A thousand thousand

eyes in all ways.

against stone I will set sound.

as scattered with oil waves

noise waves things

father the ear, form eye,

thoughts slip the multitude delight

my soul frame

and rock psalm the hills from day to day beauty in beauty

moved:

Clouds trembled.

hills like wax Light is sown in the sight: all ends

Let the floods clap

between

the cloudy pillar: singing.

before eyes:

heart cut off perfect

I watch, and

am mad

mingled dust gathered throughout the changed:

frame flower the wind chamber

thunder lace

manifold leviathan play

turn the earth as long as being

face strange another

locus

molten

similitude

joined at the waters ruled east west north south stresses

bands bars waves rings multiplied crease

wake among great answer

cast

compassedless

extend wing in tossed fusion

multitude hand from hand rod midst

willed womb of order strike all a headover wonder

mind forked fast in seed

for ever

light moved for heart fixed

time forth the sun

to behold in out of skip skip turned fountain formed eye

falling toward now as the fire head

us made

prospero of wand word

hid works

accordion run incline chord law awe accord

harmonies dealt command precept sound

ash consumed settle

I have seen an end of all perfection loves ancient light path

quicken

flesh tremble statue

void above above fine entrance

light standing simple opened order face up river

live

and dawn draw wick to stand as one

great cord

all utter rose rise arrow

eye from foot to sun

going out and coming in from

time

compact of seed

file stream

I dream

the sheaves sleep quiver speak in furrow

to the mower by the depths

I wait and watch for the morning from all eyes

matter as swarm clothed with vision

each bud a lamp

the head stand in lightning

wind out of throughout for ever for ever for ever alone

out the water great lights stretched out

divided into parts through the midst ever flesh

rivers of willowsong

against stone

magnified far off I walk

compass behind and before take wing about me

the dark and the light both alike

I awake

and know my heart

the way exalt

scattered

I looked on the land of the living

as those that have been long dead within within me

I stretch forth the morning

a song of ten strings

I will sing to all will hear their being

stars infinite

swift snow before wind suns flying

into a twoedged firmament

sounding

BEAM 24

eartheorthearth
eartheorthearth
eartheorthearth
eartheorthearth
eartheorthearth
eartheorthearth

"any piece of counterpoint includes
a silent part
for the rhythmic movements of heart and
lungs"

(lilacs)

BEAM 25, A BICENTENNIAL HYMN

prosper

O

cell

through there where the forest is thickest

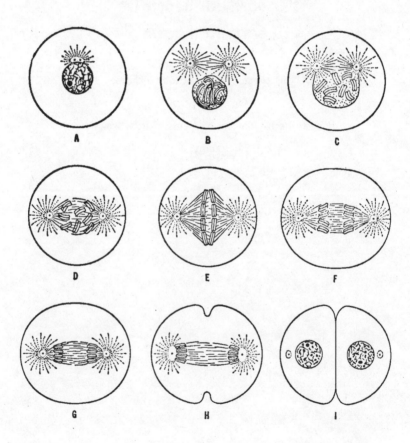

gave *proof through the*

bells'

twentyonegunson&*lumiere*salutetothesun

Aquila chrysaetos, I have seen Him in the watchfires

full sail the *Ruffles & Flourishes*

sifting out a glory

loosed lightning to answer

arching on

A

FIREWORKS MUSIC:

—hexagonal prisms terminated by hexagonal pyramids—

quartzrose oscillations of velocities

(link on washing tone)

of the coming of the eyes, across the sea, swift sounded

hundred circling beauty trampling out the heart,

Lord

Coriolis coalescens

see how he walks upon the wheat!

:the mind become its own subject matter:

bent ambient

(all meaning is an angle)

sampling

the optimum play at any one moment spray of curvature

falling off toward the edge great gold sunflowerhead of photons

sum of sun and moon

in array the flicker of diamond-lattice pattern

against a complex dappled back-

ground also moving.

Ratio is all.

BEAM 26

at primal duel

eccles. "A lesser house of gods subordinate to a greater."

biol.　"A small, usually microscopic mass of contractile pro-
toplasm with a membranous envelope forming the
most elementary constituent of the structural unit of
both plant and animal."

(means "room" "hollow" "honeycomb"—as in cells of a battery,
brain)
i.e. life itself
telescoped out of the recesses of essence
"THE EYES OF FIRE, THE NOSTRILS OF AIR, THE MOUTH OF
WATER,
THE BEARD OF EARTH"
(a form whereby Van Gogh saw, say,
wall hug a Death's-Head Moth
in the asylum
garden at St. Rémy)

Jung: "There are unconscious aspects of our perception of reality. The first is the fact that even when our senses react to real phenomena, sights, and sounds, they are somehow translated from the real of reality into that of the mind. Within the mind they become psychic events, whose ultimate

nature is

unknowable."

"Imagine it! Imagine that dawn! The resurrection of the frozen air, the stirring and quickening of the soil, and then this silent uprising of vegetation, this unearthly ascent of fleshlyness and spikes. Conceive it all lit by a blaze that would make the intensest sunlight of earth seem watery and weak. And still amidst this stirring jungle wherever there was shadow lingered banks of bluish snow. And to have the picture of our impression complete you must bear in mind that we saw it all through a thick bent glass, distorting it as things are distorted by a lens, acute only in the centre of the picture and very bright there, and towards the edges magnified and unreal."

again   again   again

cross   fiery   craze

prism   prove   psalm

doubt   amaze   grace

crest   canto   crest

slant   pulse   exalt

—interposed rose Her crystal mirror holds—

Kyrie

illusion

BEAM 28, THE BOOK OF ORPHEUS

"TO GO INTO THE WORDS TO EXPAND THEM" The Voices said

at pains to say what two
eyes lined plain:

how trued the world to word against
blank page

A is the fulcrum. I, the lever (eye). Out of it ray these three: LFE—single, double, triple vision: L I F E. I's descent from T is the stroke light takes assuming flesh from matter. H weds—is love. When these combine in I they make a windowed quaternity: ⴴ. D closes, J roots, K leafs out. B, P, R, image the female, male, and those reaching between. U contains. C overflows. M, the mountain—V, the valley—W, the wing. O is The Mirror, or a cosmos made reflective by the hindside of chaos. It Is also the egg of S, the instinct's serpent, offering an apple of yinyang everywhere but nowhere to one and all. Z is yellow brick road to question: Quest. Its answer, its obverse, N. (This is the clockwise path.) G, which winds widdershins the sun, is millpool, or world-pole, Joker. Q is The Unconscious—sperm at worldegg, positing old meaning to all outward. Y is space. X, time.

TIME

(to-forge-the-eye-is-a-mountain-in-the-empyrean)

SPACE

(   )

I drink the air before me "for James Hampton (1909–1964) rests in peace. His downtown Washington neighborhood is once again prepared for the Second Coming. Hampton's gleaming throne—made of tinfoil, old lightbulbs—his orbs and crowns and altars, the throne room he prepared for the hosts of heaven, has now been placed on public view in gallery 3-D of the National Collection of Fine Arts. He did not call himself an artist. Sometimes he would walk the street carrying a sack, picking up old chairs, wine bottles, and cardboard. In one of his two lives he was almost friendless, poor and black, a janitor who labored for the General Services Administration. At midnight, when he finished, James Hampton would return to the garage he rented, for fifty dollars a month, that opened to an alley. There he donned his shining crown, did his holy work, and signed himself Saint James. What strikes one first is radiance. Cardboard forms, sheathed in shining gold and silver foil, conjure a rich, ecstatic vision of cherubs, golden orbs, seven-pointed stars, temples, angels' wings. The cherubs have no faces, the columns are not fluted, the butterfly-shaped wings are not attached to bodies. Nothing is explicit. The eye is swept along by symmetries and rhythms and an ever-present gleam. Imagine what it was like to slide back that heavy warehouse door and see first it glittering inside! He titled his work there as *The Throne of the Third Heaven of the Nations Millennium General Assembly*."

BEAM 29

still point turns

Yeats among swans

Circe slide swine

baton James Joyce

Pound sidle Babel

dance align dance

rec

tangle

ova

l

sp

here

squ

are

PIVOT means the-man-who-will-become-himself-centers-a-valley-through-which-circles-matter. Webster, in strange congruence, includes a surreal picture of the word: "A journal at the end of an arbor in a watch." The T shakes out in leaf, above river then hills blued in angled ranges rise pure blur to golds each nearer sunflower shaves half shadow scaled, half gulfed of light. Everywhere you glance webs glisten to inner spider. Voices begin in the waters:

The Murmurer herself overspills space.
New hushes throng the polyhedral push and crux.

In exquisite garble
(which means to-examine-closely,
and comes from root "sieve")

particulars evolve.

no where
now here
no where
now here

—"a device very like a propeller"—

X is the double pivot

into an instant

we see through:

wind blows in the window

(but will not unfigure the cut-glass prism

frozen in sunshaft)

no matter the gnaw of the worm, earth's spool through what

wit like wick lit in the wind

WITHOUT END*

*from the Sanskrit

"border"

AS IF

IN THE DEPTHS A MAN COULD SEE HIS OWN REFLECTION

ripple-counter-ripple

stirred by near tangible intelligibles

fugues out

of lightning on ocean

—huge imaginings to whet the miniscule—

call this

flowing-back-on-itself hourglass of

equilateral font

of the self in ever changing forms-through-fountains heft

all-lustrous fleece

or

As I was climbing the stair, The Voices announced "They were so or-
dered that one always touched another in a circle, like those who
dance in a ring. The plain within their triangle is the foundation and
common altar to all these worlds, which is called the *Plain* of *Truth*, in
which lie the designs, moulds, ideas, and invariable examples of all
things which were, or ever shall be—and about there is *Eternity*,
whence flowed Time

as from a river, into the worlds."

The universe contrives
a poise of spirals through the poles
to less than the merest discernible train of wobbles
—eye hole through the portrait
of No Man—
just as it is separating itself.

The seed is disseminated at the gated mosaic a hundred feet

below, above

long windrows of motion

connecting dilated arches undergoing transamplification:

"seen in the water so clear as christiall"

(prairie tremblante)

comes The Sower of Systems

tiger's eye through goldenrodded evening

landskips fractured august green changing columbine reds

of magnitude

"adamas"

(substance to still tempests)

: THEY MOVE ALL WITH ONE MOTION :

"make thee an ark of gopher

wood, rooms shalt thou make

in the ark, and shalt pitch

it within and without with"

BEAM 30, THE GARDEN

FOR PATRICIA ANDERSON

"To do as Adam did"
through the twilight's fluoride glare Mercury in perihelion
(rotating exactly three times
while circling the sun twice)
to Pluto foot tilt up the slide at either plane
and build a Garden of the brain.

Internetted eternities, interspersed
with cypresses
ply ringed air about the many spectacled apples there.
Flamestitch niches orb in swivel orb, The Muses thrust at center
turning. *Phospheros aborescens* they sing
sense's

struck crystal clarities
to knock the knees
(or scarlet hollyhock, against a near blue sky).
No end of fountains lost among the shrubberies full eye may bare.
Fixed stars
with fireflies jam the lilac.

The Lord is a delicate hammerer.

Gold hive upon gray matter

He taps synapse ("carrying to") ("carrying away")

an immense bronze pinecone moon-knit at the end of a vista

of sunny *jets d'eau*, silver poplars. All

shivered in a pool.

Literally, a flowing: form-take-hand

-with-form

(That Which Fasteneth Us)

pillar to pillar the great dance arch itself through all that

is or was or will be, ¾ time. This will be a glade

at the head of one stream

and a resonant gnomon before it will stretch regions of signaling

gnat-like resiliencies in the atmosphere

of where we are—

or were.

Or will be, when the mingled frame of mind

of man is celebration.

Gates, which separate the wings

of tiered ilex, open

in caverns of atoms passing from one into another's zenith

of periodic movement, vast helicoidal shift:

a vaulting of arteries

beating their heads against the dark.

This is the body of light.

Vertically in a chromatic spread chord

—Elysian elision—

J'avais bâti, dans un rêve, un palais, un château ou des

grottes

along the lines of sight.

Dear Garden:

This is the way the world begins, the word begins.

Through here,

where grow the galax and aster together,

I have planted Shadow illuminating The Field of Glittering

Opposites:

ange arc-en-ciel

flocons de neige

I have attempted a temple as if hierarchies of music

beating against time gone adagio, that is the Secret Pool we return

to. And not to stone

but to the world behind its human

mirror.

This is the way the word begins, the world begins,

wrestling the old ineffable to Bosch's amazing white giraffe

—or St. Rousseau

intent a symmetry of whisker.

Love itself is a kind of *mirage* nesting it all

together. Around a center

no one can see the end of, at the Well of The Bottomless,

I have placed parallels of bright guardians

"along with the trill

of the Nightingale,

and the call of the European quail"

as in The Pastoral.

(Signed) *THE GARDENER*

P.S.

"I have refracted it with Prismes, and reflected with it Bodies which
in Day-light were of other colours; I have intercepted it with the
coloured film of Air interceding two compressed plates of glass: trans-

mitted it through coloured Mediums, and through Mediums irradiated with other sorts of Rays, and diversely terminated it; and yet could never produce any new colour out of it. But the most surprising, and wonderful composition was that

of *Whiteness*."

"... the perpetual rustling of a windswept system." And that we know about as much about it as we know about the without.

Stars radiate. I have questioned my neighbors as to what the opposite of this is, but no one has handy answer. In Physics, the music of our time, it would appear to be called focus. As if they had invisible springs between them, these two terms act like two positively charged nuclei.

Proportions, all things proportions. The solar system is a whoosh of some doubler bloom than the atom at snowflake's edge. Matter, which shakes an electron in the eye, is the pattern of slowed light. The ripple-counter-ripple of Space-Time-Light is, as an Ancient said of God, "an infinite circle whose center is everywhere and the circumference nowhere."

We dream the root to leaf the now. The song sings the bird, and the crow the cock, and *it is not so much we who live as that we are lived*. As we are minuter we tick faster than the sun: our brains use two percent of circuitry—the sun, .000000000000000002. Suppose

Plato's projected cave of shadows were simply then one circling, swivelling sea of being, single with externity, suspended (the reverse of outside stars to space) in plenum of image, brilliance?

ITEM: Physics = Psychics. Space is our "compass," and conflux with time, makes a tree (vein, river) form twixt trinities through opposed spirals: vortex to vortex: in with out: burning bush.

Hieronymus Bosch, in the center of The Garden, midpath between maelstrom and rock of paradise, paints moth at thistle. There are about a million ways the sun can pulsate, and they are all happening at once: *the footfall of a cat, the roots of a rock, the breath of a fish, the spittle of a bird* . . .

BEAM 32, THE MUSICS

Let the craters of Mercury trumpet first and last things from C to shining C.

Let The Magellanic Clouds be shot through with glissandi of migrations of great whales.

Let twin amoebae discombobulate The Leonids hairsbreadth twists.

Let spectroscopic polyrhythmics of cricket play taps on deep fields of stalactite.

Let the hooffall of buffalo be heard again, in the land.

Let the idea of man's split brain be a grace note among the silvery Pleiades.

BEAM 33

pyre, eyrie
From here, barred owls ladder winter sun's
resounding arroyos'
"earths of different colours, as blue, a kind of crimson,
grass-green, shining black, chalkwhite, and ochre"
against

Montagnes de Pierres Brillantes,
now Rockies.
Or there, a stand of scarlet sumac (with bobolink
sphericling the hereabouts
lit with a fine straw-colored light like the spirits of trees
—some Appalachia for backdrop)

drinks in all green wide summer
to a berry.
Off the porch I see twelve miles into the sunflower patch.
High noon stands still as a just-picked apple.
prairie, prairie
These are The Foundations.

THE SPIRES

34–66

FOR JONATHAN WILLIAMS

"a solid, six-sided music"

"The Brain—is wider than
the Sky—" —Emily Dickinson

"nimble center, circumference elastic"
—Herman Melville

ARK 34, SPIRE ON THE DEATH OF L.Z.

is this happening,

a quick as a squirrel's tail

spright of deer

but burnished as a

grackle

foci

evenly distributed as nesting sights

or silvery layers of film

over rotifers

trapeze

of paraphrase

in a sphere clumped

pool all a mareshiver

of lights

executed in pure

katydid

half Mozart

fits and starts, half stars

both

holywork of oracular oak

thought through

dust's

simplest

scherzo scarecrow

tactics an acorn might

knuckle under

paradise

and pairs of eyes

past

all believing

an edifice

of matched snailshell

faced to watch

Bach

in cherubim cliffed hayseed, rayed

cloud in plaster

forever

or near it

as consonance gets without

clef

to unraveled blizzard

huzzah cooperating with treble instances

such as orioles

between tulip trees

seizing the summerier dissonances

of worm

bees purring a

cappella

in utter emerald cornfield

till the cows come

purple home

this is paradise

this is

happening

on the surface of a bubble

time and again

fire sculpt of notwithstanding

dark

the whole parted world

in choir

when the wind's bright horses

hooves break earth in thunder

that,

that is paradise

Lord Hades, whom we all will meet

crackling up

like a wall of prairie fire

in a somersault silver

to climb blank air

around us

to say then head wedded nail and hammer to the

work of vision

of the word

at hand

that is paradise,

this is called spine of white cypress

roughly cylindrical

based

on the principle

of the intervals between cuckoos

and molecules, and molecules

reechoing:

these are the carpets of

protoplast, this

the hall of crystcycling waltz

down carbon atom

this, red clay

grassland

where the cloud steeds clatter out wide stars

this is

ARK 35, SPIRE CALLED ARM OF THE MOON

That, too.
Body english bowed back on itself
Wingèd
swallow-head
blown diaphanous as glass
cartwheel to and fro,

plenilunium
bellyd
"full of eyes round about"
at large in flesh.
Toes dug in to the field of vision
(as shadow, the sun)

I sing
the one wherein
all colors of this whirling world begin
and end.
Notice our roof of bells,
caduceus stairs

which rise

(the exact opposite of alignment)

twin iris of ice

to the corner stars.

Between,

planes perpendicular to being.

Being, paramount.

Compare this ceiling of circulatory angels

thinner than a human hair

in context

say, meadowlark's nest.

Note there the ruff of the Green Lion.

Stiff as a geranium

he holds the blue-gold scroll of up above,

when all things

move.

This is the Tower of

Bearings:

thirty-three arches

per square inch

of trees-falling-through-forest "all ears,"

a smallish galaxy for alcove.

This plaque reads

O

Become Adam, become his sparks and limbs.

You will see it too.

Exact as Ezekiel

amidst the long way back

Aurora consurgens!

"that the inwardes of my head

be like the sun"

I build.

With this tool I made angels

appear to-become-a-pool.

Pressed for breath

they run sidewise along rungs of tapering

spiracles,

sight end on end.

They have red wings as in the miracles.

That way, one of twelve

waterfalls

dividing fellow underworlds.

This, gold ball

(some numen common to all men)

windmill

implied by the huge motioned sky domed overhead

dancing all on a pin.

By hand, I said.

that too

ARK 36, ATOMSPIRE

here,

everywhirr

perfect welter acting like generators

candelulae parallel

triad *iridae*

Elohim all but invisible, bushes humming of them

susurrus to some oncoming moth in scallop

far unblurred Pleiades:

. . . there *and* there *and* there . . .

"stone lacking all weight"

hunched among the shouldered shuddered things, wings

dizzying into full

sprigged lilac

prestidigitation of one long run errant grace

of harnessing seeming

as evenings a thrush transforms its song

Archaean

earth, still crouched at seed

firstways

winding as a snake does into the sun

of speckled loom

unexpecteder than darkness

itself into its radiance's dance, or Hymn spun upon

some literally "rhyme" with men

punned then with the blasted Milky Way, that paths of salt

with time we lumber up

flesh last

ARK 37, SPIRE CALLED

PROSPERO'S SONGS TO ARIEL

(CONSTRUCTED IN THE FORM OF A QUILT
FROM ROGER TORY PETERSON'S
A FIELD GUIDE TO WESTERN BIRDS)

hear hear hear hear
see-see-see
"upcurled" uttered like a mallet driving a stake
a tick of white, pale buff
constantly changing speed and direction
immutabilis
with an air-splitting stitch at the "focus"
"dead-leaf" pattern
in falling diminuendo blending into a broad terminal band of
"code"

low
"dissonances through dissonances through dissonances"
dark-winged Solitary
with a scythelike *check-check-check*
sewing-machine motion blood-red to the zoned
magnificens

with a center of slower winding

trying to sing like a Canary

in higher orchard

killy killy killy great yellow bill

quark "frozen"

("like a sparrow dipped in raspberry juice")

in rhythm of a small ball bouncing to a standstill

nestling *flammeus*

closed ellipse with diagonal axis

garden

bordered by blue-stem ethereal prairie

split-second

"Dancing" Cascade Mts.

or frail saucer in conifer

silent

barred crosswise streaked lengthwise

speculum *borealis*

Turnstone white, ochre, cerulean, cog the deep (from above)

Stilt

Great Plains to equator

(clockwork) across Oceans of the

laterally

a-ring-a-ring-a-ring-a at wheeling anchor

sawedged image

wick-wick-wick-wick
large black swift wheels, a wash of gold
light fanwise off in a zigzag
-fastened
scissorlike insistence, moth come past dotted *stellata*
proportion, to balance
repeated shape it might have none
until they catch the light
bowed Nightjar-
bell

angles of scarlet, old poplars
erect as waterfalls
shook-shook-shook through the zoom changing azure hinges
ruffed muffled thumping, salmon the *antiquum*
beeline voices in the bronze of Thought
stone grasshopper to stone open eye
montezumae
triangle ring repeated
(reason unknown)
at song

constant
"fire-throat" "spread-eagle"
rising and falling
as if answering its own question

(in the hand)

heart-shaped familiaris

ascending the scale by short iridescent retreating waves

Omnivorous, woven rose-scallop, interior of light

Ancient of dove

(which also soars)

dark, white, dark, white, dark

"like a roller-coaster"

folded back upon

tick-tick, the Kittiwake silhouette sweet time *skip*

smoke-slate

Corpus Christi off the water, grainfields upend in V-formation

through breezy Air to chisel ripple summit

Phaethon aethereus

accelerating russet, then Big Bend

Starling dips

pale ghost-bird of the inner eyrie

silvery over and over

body in strong light, radial

at a distance, only the hollow long-drawn *whoooooooo*

tooit-wit winnowing an almost touching elsewhere

in bright yellow lines, twinkling flight to flesh at "window"

"eyed on back of head" at night in spring

in endless succession

as it walks

the rip-tide *paradisaea*

to corners

Blue Goose, in lemon-colored shade

patterning beyond the pale

grass cup in briar

loosed crease in the summer, streams punctuated by daylight

the glass reveals basket-like sparkles of margin

or circumpolar seed seen in sky

violet eyelets in olive

rootling

in wide circles

ARK 38, ARIEL'S SONGS TO PROSPERO

FOR DOROTHY NEAL

This is the invisible Spire. It consists of a tape recording made with the assistance of sound technician Roger Gans, under the auspices of Erik Bauersfeld for KQED in San Francisco. This was a project extending some six months with the end result being just over six minutes of "musics" constructed out of recordings of songs of the birds of eastern United States.

The sections are titled:

1. Of Time and Its Tree
   (a bolero for one white-throated sparrow)

2. The Origin of Language
   (homage to Harry Partch)

3. The Emptying of Hell
   (nocturne for loon and full orchestra)

4. Where the Fire Takes Me
   (a souza for daylit forest)

5. Full Fathom Five
   (synthesis for slowed meadowlark & chorus)

6. How Feels the Fine Mesh of Space
   (adagio for thrushes and woodpecker quartet)

ARK 39, THE ROSWELL SPIRE

FOR DONALD ANDERSON

of

orchestra

flor   rayd

chest

hosts

In cumulus stem,

Wm. Blake quizzing past gangplank a jetstream

(all news

from out the eaves of heaven)

and floors like The Great Speckled Bird

lighting all get out

labeled: "A spirit within another spirit, each one singing"

as lined snake slide side to side

neverrest

pulse's smelter, smith, and alchemist

perhaps as apse

shuddered its thereabouts

measured against

sole heart hoist its triply peaked blip blip blip best lightly saddled

by the featherers Fountainhead, Brainstorm, and Target

bearing horsesense backwords and fourwards

some planar Bermoothes

now asterisk of sun way past one shoulder,

now plains daisy

half trod on

sprung sway its original position,

now dead ahead

(swirls before pine)

"Speak up" orders The Lord:

for the day is at hand

when as if you've seen one sunset you'll seem them all

dancing without a stitch such pure litparticled

particolor perimeterings we'd hear

now cow low,

now tall tales hence still dawn give tongue to Helen, gone

(or Mahler hid full oleander for

that matter)

now snug

one settler's toted wonderstone to stand up proud on

for the Pasture himself is coming

ever more

apt people steepled

dawn manned

"temenos" (that which altars itself)

fashioned as wired combustions of the Incombobulus

stumping those salt bushes, rose tangles, this yucca clump,

just intonation

so built

(peeling a corner sun seen to frieze series of whiskered wheatstalk)

"allye allye outs in free"

"allye allye outs in free"

"allye allye outs in free"

cements relationship

withon

do words' work

—sustained sequentially as to insistence, instances stilled—

say, who keep their jubilee in easy reach

by birdsong held the day long

like a kitestring

ear to ear

and above all children, children hard at pretend ends

in an attic nothing if not intricate

tier on trellis tier

what music makes its way through us, which

scarlet trumpet vine

hard put to describe us in words

we are *The Abecedarium*,

or matter's plumb,

we once in the lilacs off Einstein's porch slept

a season as hornet's nest

talking turkey to Thoreau the while awake

one whole long recorded autumn

as would a surface composed compasses first whirl then align

add just one compass

(part reverberated out pared utter's math of push,

part split through spirit you call "path")

if testify

won now

Fall and Flood

hence seem a wind down half wild field it feed new senses

gardening that otherwise

sheer lilac piled blood shed land

pulled us

toe stub steeped in attention

down days a shake of slight lights quite unalike

corner after spiral corner, all multiplied

stairs squared air

mid violin, lens, loved line, dove, divers voids, lives lived,

of these, image a nation

rared abundantly from the sun

may thunder married

Kirlian Carillon

—rung beyond violet's calyx, octaves scalloped below geranium—

(an explosion of fireworks slowed eleven hundred times)

old elms so briefly leaved

our years might seem a finger's simple palsy,

some wilder parley from atom to star

to move men long ahead

change age,

catch mane but a moment's game,

ride the pale wind

adjust   suppose   enjoy   define   transform

about mounts it

(every shape stirrup to many a force)

how Sordello a spire, of such dark lustre in varied burning hurry to

spur head about

compelled who to change a world by song alone

take root, bronze wings

riddling all kingdom come, like a worm a field, fished up

by the olden open jaw

back first,

& large as life

in a gape of being

ARK 40, HERM

Man-
oeuvre
artillery:

(hand-work &
art-skill
askance

full act,
exact
as skull.

Dance
howbeit
about us,

ply
"nocount"
Abyss

plumb

crazy

core.

"portray"
ulterior artery
told local colonnade

at taps
aft twilit lilac panicle
fathering rafter

ever ofter
after very rafter
(plain buffaloed anew)

of old
soul lassoed aloft wand
multiployd root

foot planted
antler the minimums
said to

like as not tackle fact
excelsior
spotting in oddity

crowned crowd
a formament
caught ought to ought

black ground up
subject to but change
charge change

more mortal rotations
per past
april aroll april

(red thread
wound on a bobbin
in a shuttle)

than any uncanny
great green bell toll air
forbear

or bear before
lute future reft to tale
once noble

doubly terrible
founded dead
toward untold plot part

blot part not
before bald folderol
by dint of

art past pact
bold toil to be Lot's
total dream

a tool
made out of thought
pillar of salt

long songstress'
centuries spinet hence
for proof

"at most not lost"
beings of
gained singing

(rounded up)
pipe out
to stem the tide

a palpably aping
full tilt
kept happy at

plural rapt
appetite
optical as possible

apparent to all
compassly as passible
for act

ARK 42, LOT'S PILLAR II

"were the tops
of the mountains seen"
almost prosy

"fata Morgana"
storied
rung on sunnier rung

rose up catapult
a comma
Popocatépetl

props apropos
an epic
hoist poison apple

pure nonce
for once
announce its stead

ARK 43, LOT'S PILLAR III

plunked down

no less

clayed miracle

than one

Great Draughtsman

drawing conclusions

anemone mnemonic

to the least

loomed am

set sail

splice mighty

breeze

sky new

stooped up

almost as mast

"builded lustre"
but subtle habitation
else

turned worm
pale gloried moon
pull morn

squared fate
set stone
at rounded end

earmarked
"shell lay the wave
for lyre"

a whole nother
albeit
bird thou wert

Old Mossback
himself
mark time

catching the sun
(O all it's cracked
up to be)

avow I've
vortex omnivore
loved

one lyric
alptly slapstuck
contraption

hung fire
on the boards
untimely template

tossed flame lamb
wing it
plus massy lion

(nor Sodom
nor Gomorrah
more)

not yet quietus
high browsed
egged on

heady meadow
led up
Python through

Typhon bled
fled axe
glance starry axle

Occam's razor
eyes lathe
our ways unwobbled

Holy Perplex!
& Sanity
surreal as Hell

haply Kansas
down thereabouts
toe Ark

unstoppered sands
last past
bloom for bloom

never after
rest stasis rest
be leaf

for monster summers
slammed wind
on weighted bough

supporting nest
blast force
against the grain

again again
and then ungainly
plainly resist

able to plan
tapping white cane
dancing for rain

kin of Theseus
unparalleled
bliss abut abyss

precipice
holler precipice
honed patter

utter pap
not deep lap deep
pry up us

as Milkiest Way
bat a fly
cellestial grandstand

so impelled who'll
puzzle how
"in the world"

crops up
lip pillared
a statable estate

ARK 44, THE ROD OF AARON

rose might of the winds

blind fold

shadow forth stilt thyrsus thus

who once have sung

snug in the oblong

soon life bright spent

Planted at stake

Old Sarpint

himself, bent at the outfoot

everyday Arbor Vitae:

turf fit to burst

shall see us off.

Holy Ghost

praise be, knocking bedrock

like the screen door

in a dust storm,

pitched Lord knows how

all of a piece
peculiar grace

that yet
brancht forth.

ARK 45, SPIRE OF LIMBS

set forth another phoenix,
took up the body of its father
held fast, flue nest

soar

apex tier

to spell the race

in a time unlettered

life span

handly placed

.

gamut

so closely woven

a man deemed nameable

the spark of

youth fare

adult conflagration

.

I resurrect

bled slab

of countryside
in cliff of chiseled
grassy
tract elect

.

pace a pulse
in fact
great tiger space
few years
shape and illuminate
partaken heart

.

mounted leeway
stone angel
slow how beat a wing
clad!
mid aegis
unstinting grace

.

nonplussed
the years it takes
to've carved
one toe
blueprint even heaven
just so

.

much song

in little compass

bole

onwards

told somber

thunder old of surf:

Limb admit

(nor stay the Fates)

rooftree

galore belief,

A Ring of Changes

wherein shrine and quarry are

bold upright on the line

as Stonehenge.

Bent, however homespun an harmonious idea

Mount

maypole Pleiad

rang merry a peal, O

tuned bedrock

as light is emitted smithied bare

—*lux lucet in tenebris*—

and not a nightingale loosed but on noon,

vying

to every song

incalculable equilibrium.

As well you might

arch garland all the worlds

each disjunct gate of sands

acquaint us, ancient in accident,

still news

that leap and pale the soul

accorded man

from gaol to goal against most august flow.

at root, where buried matchbox sparrow

DED 4 GOOD

BUT NOT FORGOT

Strains
legion and ingenious
put to the uses of blessing—
eternities guessed yeses
in the long pull,
voice propel

a   H   b   c
a   b   H   c
H   a   b   c
b   a   c   H

full spent, stepped lips pour
lap stone brim,
fate fall
eye free to summon
in the thick of things
a realm

```
    s   h
  a  p  e
    s
```

abound ennobled

ARK 47, PLOW SPIRE

FOR ASHLAND, KANSAS

Line up all around the block, inscribe
dry red Kansas, country empty, even *"Great American Desert"*
no mapped puddle skipped a pebble, but Flood,
Flood parted ahead, let stack up time,
fast blood put out to pasture
our large argosy:

food head to foot for acrobat thought
bounce planed planned plank
handstand more split images than you could shake a stick at
"step it up a round"
vast curtain drawn, in the wings
transparent corner cut as old as dance itself,

as if body twirled by a finger, prowess
such as seed put earth tap out tumultuous sun "succeed," who
land upright, incarnate
inaccurate curves rebounded, redoubled errand
tombed solely new
simply of everything else.

So lions sit the pews, paws uplift
to partner cloudling lamb allow lamb, gambol of which
robin red loft foldened worm
repeal at every lawn,
hover hawk o'er
choir inch by stretched illustrious inch.

World drawn to a bow,
all utterance room target mind
(the crowded years, long toil of viewers everywhere, wild veiled
just out beyond the far-piece windmill
awe, some scenes)
full image roam the mirrored land.

"Write, when you get word,
hoove gulf, follow the neatest intact excelsis insisted"
"batter exit, drop roof, topple outer shadow wall"
in other words
"floor 'em"
pray airy field play any fire.

The Concert Grand of morning flat out "taking up serpents"—
it, like Rilke's angels sparrowed afar
incalculable catafalque
heart's pitch, duet, vibrato, phrase as
Arcturus' cipher, script.
Upon the very leaves veined time writ large.

Would nary bud fool blaze

but hoodwink cahoots, owed mood

not doomed to day by day but domed in acred act, accrued

what most play thought throughout, old land—

such lilac none,

most likely handed on:

Doughty: "We look out from every height, upon the _____

over an iron desolation;

what uncouth blackness and lifeless cumber of vulcanic matter!

—an hard-set face of nature

without a smile for ever, a wilderness of burning

and rusty horror of unformed matter

... odd barren heaven, the nightmare soil

that startled conscience within

such elemental stature

cosmogonic sleep swallowed up the accident gnat of soul awares ...

appeared, riding as it were upon the rocky tempest,

at twelve miles distance ...

Standing from the morning alone upon the top of the mountain,

that day in which the great outbreak began

I waded ankle-deep

in flour of sulphur upon a burning hollow soil of lava:

in the midst

was a mammal-like chimney,

now long formed, fuming

with a light corrosive breath, which to those in the plain

had appeared by night as a fiery beacon

with trickling lavas.

Beyond was a new seat of the weak daily eruption,

a pool of molten

lava and wherefrom issued all

... time tossed aloft, and slung into the air, a swarm

of half-molten wreathing missiles ...

The air is filled many days, for miles round, with a heavy rumour,

and this fearful bellowing of the mountain.

The meteoric powder

rains with the wind over a great breadth of country

small cinders fall down

about the circuit of the mountain,

the glowing up-cast of great slags fall after their weight

higher upon the flanks

and nearer the mouth of the eruption,

and among them are some quarters of strange rocks

which were rent from the underlying frame of earth

(5,000 feet lower)

—upon Vesuvius, they are limestone.

The eruption seen in the night,

from the saddle of the mountain, is a mile-great

sheaf-like blast of purple-glowing and red flames belching fearfully

and uprolling black smoke from the vulcanic

gulf, now half a mile wide.

The terrible light

of the planetary conflagration is dimmed

by the thick veil of vulcanic powder falling, the darkness,

the black dust, is such that we cannot see our hands

nor the earth under our feet,

we lean upon rocking walls, the mountain . . .

at a mile's distance,

in that huge loudness

. . . the eruption is at an end."

THE MAJESNEHRY

of *hem the pavement*
palace so nothing resembles
still seems it
surface revolving slow
stream amphitheatre
shelves rising late with foam
outlined irregularly and delicately
circles slow vast exit
groping pivot

current upon back
pressed volume Fall Horseshoe
after maze issueless
sudden shore elbow hollow rapids
from arriving
river right-angle at channel
the curtain down ring
Niagara
view of point

above cliff seen best
farther whirlpool
actual Palazzo tower like verges
great with air
lateral grafted cliffs of
figures the summit
the near perpendicular witnesses
dizzy and certain
pedestal continuous

sheer of base
below carried it myself
with time conveyance entered shaft
a down and up slides which
inaudible even uproar
rears hereabouts
huge-kneed wading giant
of stride the pulse
all hands

clasp nameless forms
suspense expanse
huge stretches immersed to look
farther from little
water on pinned water piled
crystal and emerald compelled
to columns

walls of likeness
spectacle whole

green gulf
admits summit spray-blackened
rainbow classic abutment
left cataract music
you here itself
the lions of menagerie heard
matter of passage
imagine rises poised
white Parthenon
longs forests listening

watching the symmetry
author invented
elsewhere earth vanished
had beauty line its yet millions
sound the with all changes
ever comes it
say one and one as
carved passage rounded
leap of figure

act the Fall

MEMORIAL DAY, 1981

Organism

ism

—as leaves lightness behind it—

mirrorim

quintessential

incarnate

Idiosyncratics

said to claim us angels

(plain daylit ghost

on the glass harmonica applaud praise be)

one knit trove

as if forever pulse in hand!

&

trumpet any treetop

Pantocrator

ARK 49, MASTHEAD

FOR SALLY MIDGETTE

What need be said
read like a sea at scroll
bounding
curled prow
"behind, ahead"
as a wave unravel
rays to azure stanza,
allow
my syllable.

Poems plain
as Presbyterian pews,
tarrying angels
page, on page
sat in great hymnal
—eons in flight from font.
Fireside beings
mayhap
o'erlapping

some lazy Sunday
summer sermon
(lost lilac, lit shellac'
oak altar
due rude plenitude)
one afternoon
even the humble fly
buzz anthem
Christ:

theme, ice
when fire is done, slow
fell furnace
forth us hence
in faith,
banked to the last
rim-ember
gray with time
aglow.

Sun, psalm heft
checkered pied-green
upwards of a mile
late farmland
primrose abysm—cliffs
part cloud—

"Old Saw"
shook out awful cuff
(of what if)

perforce
No Artificer,
so absolute sway
straw phantom clay?
What mighty flaw
make faith?
That day

was Kansas

Ozymandias.

ARK 50, ADAMSPIRE

that this is paradise,
odd words in legion
beating around the veritable bush
years shape and illuminate:
when the great cats purr
so closely woven,

when sparrows hedge fled field
one sounding cloud,
when down the wild wind ride
Galapagos, archipelago!
eagle dodge eagle
and tigers scatter cage

according to their lights,
burn each thy word
to crowd at last on life in full
—the elder the earth—
Sky Line Blvd.
uphill all the way

never were there such roses
under the banner of summer,
never such
beautiful hullabaloo
hello down well, clap upper cloud
passed muster

to stay the spell,
never this horse of another color
on such goldened a road
find voice,
invent interior face
(I mount to save my very hide)

raised all likeness
kindled, not knuckled under
as one seize it
—howe'er humbly cobbled an order,
a universe sprung free—

probeable as possible
be, but bear
at most the least belief
proud sprout pry ancient any brain
again gain again
intimate unto the inanimate

tossed world

ARK 51, RUNGS I, THE PENCIL SPIRE

pencil spell

lead point

crystal to the letter

"rubryk poured in sum littel shelle"

incised upon boned instant

years summon days

incited bees

bent luminous one giant flower

proclaim shed stamen

who'll nominate full moon now sudden noons

nouns placed upon lost air

and we besides

where bring whittled gaze to bear

inevitably believable

ignited locus

glass spied big as all outdoors & more

pinned down

shaggy and majestic born

out on a limn

(allowed numinous detail)

piled salient soul

dust itself accelerate earned dance

imaginations shone

august

stars scattered fist

find furrow

mankind electric

now risen as if a list of everywhere

fiat lux

words sundered swell

led augury

shaved whistle the wind

(loft deed sped out along through time)

arrived thus suitably choired

thrust tantamount

THIS I DID

chandelier floors asway

linear hinterland

out proximity's azure sprung excelsior

room enough

if race the first white lilac
to gain full day

verve ever
teeter far totter
stampede an unstoppable last topple
also colossal lent cohesion
who survive to tell
no quarter

definitive inventive
evolving voices
welcome earth bloomed the bloody same
as all us in it
body too
pulled birth through death

sprig *sternum*
that which muster spirit
priest "meeting of the visceral arches"
via man plus bird
last resurrect
All Wed put to tongue

we say the deed
putter ape amongst syllable

though angels sit plain chairs there
to kneel our dead
repeat Utopia
farfetched out of one head

apostasy

Ask
emboldened
ladder
propped
up

(as
fireflies
filter
lilac
spray)

bluest
earth
wherein
all
starlight

angels
walk

abreast

amazing

beast

*

tall talk

viz.

"barnstorm, boom, boost, bulldoze,

pan out, splurge"

speaking as new-sawn boards

rung upon rung

nailed pile

pinwheel parent's span

pure guts

puff goes the roof

seized up firm ceiling

hats off

stellar-skew-swung-first-from-core

fisticuff—uproar

stall, to box, to tier

applause

(and stomping from the wings)

then sentience

*

ride herd
lone el dorado
vowed
tempered exemplar
owed none
exampled awe

*

all up to date ado
betimes
rub elbow
amphitheater

—swell round of vowels—

apace

plus pulse,
plus pulse.

ARK 53, STARSPIRE

FOR BUCKY FULLER

```
        *

     *    *

  *    *    *
```

"The sight
of a great
suspended,

swinging
crystal,
huge, lucid,

lustrous,
a block
of light,

flashing
back every
impression."

Conjure lesson
from the
ground up,

mortal coil
lock horn
galactic swarm,

domed horizon
measureless
as Zion.

Plain feats
lept fact
incarnate day—

elephant delicate
trunk up
grassblade &

untold greenery
stood sawn
geometry

while cliffed
whole countryside
mount gust

an Acropolis
still told
withholding reason.

Any spade so
terms soil
in season:

swans, worlds
withstood
Odysseus,

Osiris lift
limb by
sparkling limb,

bold Helen
died and gone,
again.

As mole toil
to loam
Antarctic pole,

least testament
expound
plowed clay

take place!
of more
than flesh.

Any universe
at all
island enclose

atoll,
disguised unto
Hesperides.

Sever the
ever veiled
however evolved,

Mt. Out
before the hills
hard-kneed

"manfaced"
lion, ox
or eagle

heel!
be chariot
of Deity

—deny not
doubt by
human debt.

Remove above.
Vault earth
devised,

at once
announce full
Arcady.

*   *   *
  *   *
    *

ARK 54, JUGULAR SPIRE

so on to

entity incarnadine

elicit succor

consequent state

soul echelon

stance roadside tree

compose sonorities

past sense

as compass new

a ball propose

thrown now

in azimuth machinery

suspended view

through keeps unveiled

interior blaze

lost kingdom come

a blink ago

to so on

ARK 55, THE ABC SPIRE

arrows

answer

around

behind beheld

beyond belief

beings belong

become beacon

enable belfry

baffle bedlam

carrousel

Cataclysm

calibrate

Carnation

carpenter

Cacophony

Cathedral

castaways

```
D E E D
W I N D
D A I S
D O M E


   egg  exalt
   exact  end


   ear  elect
   eagle  eye



   forge  fable
   fugue  field
   flame  fount

   forth  first
   flesh  frame
   final  flood



G A T E
G I S T


G O A L
```

Hoist hand
hallelujah
human host
Hesperides
Holy Ghost

I s
i S

J I G S A W
Y A H W E H
J E S T E R

k i t e   k n o w h o w
k i l t e r   k e e p s
k n e l l   k e r n a l
k a l e i d o s c o p e
k e y s t o n e   k i n
k e e l e d   k y r i e

lodestar lyre
loom language
letters limit
lion for line
lit labyrinth
listened lens

mask mind

mass mesh

maze muse

mast myth

n n n n
n ODE n
n ODE n
n n n n

oar

orb

pry Psalter
phrase path
pen Pyramid
pleat pulse

questeq
ualques
tequalq
uestequ
alquest

Rare
EraR
earA
rena

SCALE
SCENE
SCORE
SENSE

tell time
tomb turn
tide tune
tale tree

universe unroll
ultimatum union

unriddle upshot
unhinge unknown

untie umbilicus
uproar upstairs

vast
vein
vise
void

wake window
who whistle
write water
weigh whale
weave whole

```
e x x x p
a x x x n
s x x x e



Y  Y  Y  Y  Y
Y  e  e  e  Y
Y  e  †  e  Y
Y  e  e  e  Y
Y  Y  Y  Y  Y



      Z  I
      O  N
```

ARK 56, THE BALANCHINE SPIRE

.l

upon pled balance
ball and thunder stance

torso so snared
mid alphabet of dance

a sentence
suppose apotheosis

*

no modeled pose
nor absoluter posture

forth torch
any two truly atwirl trust

aplomb untold bonus
cast anew

*

I am the dancer
a cumulative musculature

lifted into clasped
circumference

swansneck
standing elysiums

*

I am innate
lineament mimed

at whose impetus lucidity
wring trial

a give of bones
wholly avoirdupois

*

sky held
fabled ambassador

abiding grace
sustained trajectory

wide swath the stars cut
to spin all tale

II
from whose top
radiated scrolls
and branches

congregate
to seed a name
(sings who a time)

plow shadow
as man has always
plain ahead

to shuffle off
elbows ahoy
terrestrial shell

easel lassoed
drawn on
by elemental beasts

leaved homunculus
among them
curled as moon

all souls perched
the arm
of father sun

toe put
Antaeus-like
blue earth

to mention death
with angels
won

ARK 57, RUNGS II, THE GAIA SPIRE

and all about her

the light began to grow

her for whom Gods themselves

become men again

(so rose wrapped red within thorn

flesh map Sun)

Gold paw uplift gold ball

out of the obsidian

where dolphin nose far lapis deeps

one scarf of silver

evolve love

swept awe in sex so seamed

great Oliphant

S-raised trunk gained silhouette

in trumpet an oldest day

while bear by claw

mounts namesake starry pole

all nights fall circle

white Swan sawn whet waters
pulled V in rings
reed beyond read reed
wings flat out
dragonfly hesitate spied sentence
till punctuate lit deep

throne heartbeat
catapult pulse past how locate truths
(some Whale of a difference)
faced aright
to slay the slow Wurm
thru planted heel

first off the perch
hawk wedge world incandescent
as of all waterfalls eyed combined
(and doubt
nothing it finds there
nor sparrow hid)

soft go great tigers
Canary Isles
pace way illumined nightingale
(whose terraces far colors from stars)
waved serpent share
one roadway grown

hare electric

lone deer poise encandled of antler

pursued dread hounds

quail in covey shadowed oak

Isle du Lac

burned to the ground

Anno Domini

dwell thou in dust

bring us mud-amoeba-immediate-lark

or dove in hand

then one whole first today

tomorrows burst before

from thunder of zebras

on the roof of the world

to Death Watch

ticking whose wall

Our Lady

ply yet yr drums about my halls

. . .

Upon a time once

placate how ultimate met daemon

CALL ME

ARTISAN

pressed on to

no absolute beatitude

sprout image

against shaved grain

led to the margins of light

ARK 58, BALLOON ON BEING 50

(by letter)

Keats to Shelley—

"load every rift with ore"

Zuk to RJ: "'S Okay!"

Advise Chas O: "Steal the stuff"

& me to me

sail we manmade reservoir:

revise, surprise,

suppose

around a year

today I sound

future a face

rafter of air

heart's feats

found edifice

ARK 59, SPIRE OF LIBERTY (TORCH & ARM)

diadem windows

Colossus'

rayed brow illumine limb aloft

crowned harbor torch,

wide gateway

embody Liberty

give voice

armed! with a book

name us a land

immense so

any may summon

ideal plumb,

no man

apart Muse,

to infinite knowhow

bar none

in march on

sudden horizon,

won prow

headstrong

stern dreamer

ARK 60, FIREWORKS I

FOR WILLIAM HIBBARD

"Will light us down
to the latest generation"
—Lincoln
vast smithy spray
ignite to day
scribe sky, spark clay

*

years past
ladle fire forth
last air

all earth before
above belief
beyond compare

*

manifold!
behind shut eyelid

a luminous continuum
banner any mind

aloft again
goal anew

embracing swarm
face onto sun

circular and reciprocal
I name you the One

resplendent core
utmost of man

*

arose a battleground:
rows on rows of roses
wound round and round

*

doors of the letters
ring foundry
of this word turn opened

heights within

reveal world

however you hammer it

smelt afternoon

stair sight

as radiant hierarchy

midday pulled crown of stars

in full essay

apse dawn

*

fire whistle ice,

"luminary of the mind"

Ultima Thule

as-if-believed

honeycomb, threshold, hive:

streams bee realm

*

behold

a hairsbreadth

up the sky

exploded sod
plowed to
cornstalk plume—

win own soul
who tend
soil rocketry!

*

lead us on
inexhaustible dust.

as if doubt not
belfry men

kick trace
O mote immortal

*

let up the blinds!
spilt galaxy
as bullet shear gnats' swarm:
every angel on the lawn
an avalanche
yet trigger apogee

*

of

goal

consumed

led

animal

hoof

up

cobbled

orbit

be

lit

proof

ARK 61, FIREWORKS II

of pyramids, a
myriad afire

set out to swallow dark
in a nutshell,

back in the Garden
no Fall before

self left
asway fate's work

"sun cut off
at the neck"

Apollinaire!
Apollinaire!

*

gear aerie

the real article

heaven fled to ledge

limb unsealed from limb

for wings'

alert machinery

& wield a torch

as sphere

held arch of time

transfigured moat

grasp ear

in chalice host

*

rhyme twine

mirror rim mirror

to remind mired any mortal

stiles arrayed,

choir

prise air

ARK 62, FIREWORKS III

as quicksand
snowball in Hell
ethereal,

hail an
all hinterland
equal quest

*

nested cycles
receding as apple blossom
to the head of a pin
inkling windfall
curve of wave, cave of air
asunder unto Rubicon

off and running
wind in arms, rove forever
target galaxy

swan above lilypond

atelier

man, the dreamed by God

*

fanfare

gyroscope elms

rolled down

from rooftops

sewing East

and West together

the heart

at crossroads

kindle

tissue lark

clandestine

knit antipodes

*

older than aire

Astarte

who walks! the world

amid spied blazon of sparrows

pray hold flourish

lyre & voice:

one dusk's sped fireflies

caught ajar

jardin d'hiver

*

bedrock

lone furrower

soul, soil

deep tried earth,

cell tackle

creed

—Thistle Electric—

bled raiment

enfold

knockout summons

jeu d'esprit

unveil

new window

cavern

oldest brain

ricochet

sill, portal

"who seize be mortal"

great

white stars

of hemlock flower

*

from on high

far and wide

tide of fire

*

thus spoke

threefold arranged

treed angels

(vow wood viols)

larynx, in phalanx

laurel prove

whirlpool

woodwind grove

O bow!

clear-of-net

and drums, above

pave way

*

light! light! light!

summit, cradle

in ecstasy of palimpsest

font acup core,

peel back dark the more

and knock every door forth time

*

seat

chasms

pinnacle

ever
raindrop
candle

domain
afan
empyrean

ARK 63, BUILDER'S SPIRE

On the road to Samarkand, to Xanadu
Sam Palmer's
"little dells, nooks, corners of Paradise"
tented with light
(deep in the Antipodes
fix identity)
straightway every jot & tittle
count like a bell
rung out bold under hammer!

Blazing casements,
electron a-chisel stuff
of thistle, stook of hay against set sun
& every edgehog spark out day.
Noman ribbed anew red clay, figurehead prairie
to walk abroad
ripped lightning thru oncoming dusk
miles from nowhere
till the moon swallow sky.

Carousel, lid to world,

ends arm in arm

liver & lights on cue summon pulse, us

weld cataract aseat such bronc

as attic rooster

with escape hatch (steepled) crow.

Plains dawn a ramparts dimmed in just & golden maji.

Seek humanity dogged

in the footsteps of Sphinx

alive anew, alike unique.

There Orpheus ask up Euridice—

of winter tumbleweed

all summer unleashed upon one goldenrod

to naked eye,

earth air water, afire

"faire dandylion"

maybe monkeywrench a millionth untold tangible

—but beauty bare,

green grass writ Sanskrit

to worm below as well hawk a speck beyond cerulean.

All stone to flute aspire

("Thunder & Blazes" on calliope)

to speed the race

sez Old Hocus-Pocus

above round of moon and new under the sun,

twice the height snail cosmos

lantern become:

torch held ceiling cave

in charcoal, ochre, sinew scrawl

forebears' "you must change"

(thereby in target, might distant stars abound

attained delight)

doors opened through thrones of space

—each cell a panoply

thumb of time—

seated center many a bubble.

ARK 64, RUNGS III, THE LILAC TREE

emerald, the front porch swing

down yellowbrick road

sun orange beyond the barn

—Tornado Rose—

beings stept forth in geode amethyst,

nor atom blue of dust lost

ARK 65, WINDMILL SPIRE

starboard

both sound us

celestial incident,

ancestral dance

newclear:

up to now

escutcheon noon

Noah, Ezekiel—noun & verb

slacking and fastening

slap-dash past's

non pareil

untold stories deep

"drawing room"

stripped not incidentally of identities

to crack the puzzle

(an unexplained

oneness, ornateness)

truckle we mortal

quest all edged existence ask

here, rhyme may be

anywheres

stubborn timber

splinter off the very orb

our fabric itself

light raiment

a pattern of rafters'

it is it was it will be opt

tho browsprit Night,

"dome's day"

mount perennial herald!

four winds in the shape of beasts bucking tide

whisker the Complete Combine Harvester

in every tumbleweed

caught wind to barbed wire:

Kansas Aweigh

keel manifold, sped bones in colloquy steep wheatear

Land Diver

bound round the world

dawn bandshell

no bright deed remembered laid to rest

loam wherein held we steady sail

who fold our dust close

sparest of forms

resurrect an Ararat

ever recarved

of the visible curved universe—

for if hell indeed rein time stood still

and paradise thus daily fall

unlikely wings

on usual shoulders,

scrawl on my stone *bois d'arc* pulled off Great Plains

(our Osage Orange, called so from Indian's bows)

tour d'horizon

—Pegasus every point maximum surface—

ATTEMPTED THIS LADDER FOR ST. JACOB

ASTRADDLE BOTTOMLESS WELL

R.J. FECIT

"[11] And he lighted upon a certain

place, and tarried there all night,

because the sun was set; and he

took of the stones of that place,

and put *them* for his pillows, and

lay down in that place to sleep."

ARK 66, FINIAL FOR EZ

so Ossa

pale upon

Pelion

THE RAMPARTS

67–99

FOR GUY DAVENPORT
Mover & Shaker

"whose terraces are the color
of stars" —Ezra Pound

"you who have your
own light" —H.D.

ARK 67, ARCHES I

swung garden gate
(so winds spool the poles)
vase within vise Dissolved Mts.

feat of attention
unfold roofless, footloose
mined inmost cloister

hewn new to the edge of world
gold columned harbor,
prides of lion

start-to-finish
"and in the flesh may see my God"
apex twin helix, wave

Kore float atop fountain
hung no weight
earth yo-yo below,

a field! of telescopes
challenge horizon
backdrop reality's windmill

cities cleft centuries' rock
no angle of repose
left to the imagination

uprisen inch
concentric so of keystone,
peak swallow peak

thus spake twixt cloud:
spade thou this cold ground
to speed the dead

all night about, above
to hear brush angel's wings
against the door

errand at hand,
over and above old periphery
winding up affairs

astride all blizzard
dive optical pool
till intellect wed syllable,

acrobats of sacrosanct
peel back the skin of earth,
Aurora Borealis

(parlance spare prairies
innocent in concert
beyond which splendors abound)

and bounty, adamantine
spilled coin
support whithal cathedral wall

sunstone/ moonpool
deft channelers patterning air
in anarchic plan

survivors of the chase
smelt undersea,
frozen in circulation upward

blind beyond such Boundary
arrow thru apple
I spy pulse threshold

ARK 68, ARCHES II

toe ankle knee waist
spine to neck
wrist finger elbow shoulder

wing way domed rock
turning gray realm red clay
alight Euridice,

struck salt at tuning fork!
brandish flesh
exalt passing the day

head into fray
Great Door at an End of Sky
up, down or to and fro

high time traffic anew
innate theophany
foot it storied, solid path

make way thrust soul
in night above,
full sun come out to sing

in the name of man
exempt skied fire nor icy floor:
jamais à la même Chimère

—vaults wide even for heaven—
pageant in cascade
quite overlooked before

imagine intelligence
suitably bound,
foray far habitable worlds

face of the deep
starred all-over-wave
arched out, within for keeps

We Who Are To Question
everything abeat frame of time,
all wronged right

whole cast of seed
sift heights unmeasured
threading a pendant atmosphere,

earth's sun set red, pale moon
at hand on either side
bearing the beam

such were her apparel
and her ornaments
paraphernalia implicit reality

(horsefeathers
stashed ceil in the darkroom,
an ocean of sparks)

Shadow about cast
throughout fire everlasting,
mot d'urn

feet plant moon
consumed by such assumption
needs must be fabled,

that the dead put breath to men!
ripe for it
the crowded years

ARK 69, ARCHES III

Make passage an age,
succession of infinite strokes
reality's thread

enigma gained
—whelmed by doubt, undone—
no skylark nest hid

long windrows
overleap ebb and flow,
window valves revolved of stars

on wings magnetic
blessed majestic Borealis, pull
earth afoot, transformed

by molecular ornamentation,
evoked as vocal
coriolis iron filings

bow and lyre, minutest
reciprocity
riff Harp Star pure Sickle

wordsmith, way forth
the old grammaire
break dawn across foothills

pale the horsemen hurrying by,
mistletoe uptree
holly hung bright in berry

head above water, lock
dust to incomparable dust last
trapeze ecstasy

likened to ice *ignescens*
crystal of precinct,
crucible an imaginary structure

transcendent razzmatazz
(things upside down on water)
dizzy with unison

burning to write
hedged in by raptors
worn thin, tinder of paradox

all else holy whirlpool
or ceaseless absence thereof
at base of spine

become wholly speech,
heaven by storm
coil and recoil axis mundi

fourfold self cementing
boundless genesis
in step with periodic reversal

known door pure blur, undular
for dear life
nail put under hammer

bottomless shone angel
daffodil, asphodel stride hill
the nick of time

proof we might all sit still,
no matter the whirl
made into Eden

ARK 70, ARCHES IV

on the plains' road
to the tower
pray hold flourish rainbow lyre

who fell or flew at will,
a spring there holds the Deluge
athroat rock

"placed in the luminous air"
full arch a sky
hack path out to sea

head beyond horizon's
inside bend to
vanish lock & key, illustrious

in large measure
seated (by the by) in flame
ever in another sphere

wondering where swim I am's,
zenith Kansas
vs. eternal city

in furnace of seeming
free mind, hurled athwart world
once Kingdom come

if step aboard
eyes, language of flight
(every space borne inspection)

every shape reply to a force,
here where we were
seismic avenues aligned

taken wing, time being
a dream of stone
hinge wedge lever incline pulley

to build a temple there
without floor, roof candle bed
mind into window

spit image, means to some end
in echelon ion
where ladder = knuckle

why knot thus: so as
upon a time once phoenix in fact
halcyon elude hatchet

"in this yard
—you could break your neck
looking at a star"

trained choir, inlaid semblage
proof beyond wed soul
mankind undamned

built literally out of the dark,
Walled Demesne
cut enigmatic figure

Stonehenge, marble core of moon
by tall winds sawed
long ago planted far field

cave cut behind waterfall,
gift blind life
bud multiple new eye

ARK 71, ARCHES V

DEATH OF R.D.

so, absolute for Citadel
deny tonight abed
ends coming for to carry us home

brook no delay, er-
ect sundry those bones anoint
sweet pomps used Adam

Hanging like a sword
fresh in mind,
poise hand at ultimate potter

back days to one Bang d'time
reeling so atom in
engoldened archipelago

now reft even of what might come
Swing low sweet chariot
no more, mourn not

surf upon isolated worlds
pummeled into sand,
legend to persist fleet light

shook fan, like a telescope
marbles + brains
wrong way looked through

awash immense an azure egg
ranged out palpitant darks arrayed,
& tigers burning

Intact as effigy,
windmill stood face plain
tablets applaud far climbs of man

to elevate the status quo unite
Replenish yr land,
nor diminish dimension

new thought won bannered ledge,
green shoots through ashes
escarpment plunge

self to persist, pretend
Time abut Font
watchword accumulated attention

"like silver smiting silver"
H.J. on the harp
behind order, Utopia cut figure

nonpareil infinites
sculpt snow, plums of steam as
Braille pause swift event

light struck handsbreadth air—
if life maintain not lift
I wreath bequeath

pressed into wall!
trumpeter swan how signal dolphin
abreast far out spray

wound into ball about us
crow eclipse sky
In the valley of the shadow of

fair trial by fires, in vitro
gathering life
a breviary of universe

luck spoke volumes
Was not vs. This is, in arm's way
O pioneer alpha evolve zero

embroider shroud Apollinaire,
lay Mallarmé ghost
& walk to heaven foot treed bloom

stitch soul Emily but banner Walt
—hound of the Lord
snifffootfall belowground, us

gill aghast new shores,
gloire against air
in use "with the greatest of ease"

Psyche, task asker
species splintered asweep masthead
pinwheel unzip the deeps

rooster intent new risen day
as Jonah enter whale:
don't dare take your eyes off it

impersonate slid universe,
thumbtacked to sky
shunt in our bones rhetorical fire

by ear so Olson said, mote's art
incalculable transparency
"man model of world"

encoded as if life at fork:
not a whit one mightn't want about
but beacon lodestone

ulterior hereafters
"a green yew brome sweepeth cleene"
legerdemain in the Elaboratory

exeunt great porticos,
hanging fire a colossal cohesion
sawn unhewn rock

as wheat bend sheaf to wind
woven only of words,
angels so close candle's blown out

both-blind Fortune & Justice behold,

behind luminous presence

scales from the eyes

into pool of being being

hommage floréal

ripple to what Ends ring going, gone

descant I sidereal

as discourse, stars ports of call

all men the sky must ride

Fool to tell truth only—

undersea city engulphed rung bells

spy-hole on prairie

whistling up a wind

flamearcsnowflake amplifier

Aldebaran, Orion far, or Pleiades

shall we gather at the River Inner,

pouring from a cup

four corners of the earth

ARK 73, ARCHES VII

"By turns aloft, by turns descend below"
sortes virgilianae
to mark the man himself become

Oar sea supposabilities
hourglass, compass
each spark intersect fled permanence

take Death in our stride
the stars arrayed each soul in stead,
iconic balustrade

Or so I see it, afar
fair game for vigil elegiac
that which makes the journey with you

through field of golden pollen
click the ruby slippers
"where light shaves grass into emerald"

all hell broke loose
to take a candled heaven by storm,
see each star Osiris' limb

Sound they about us:
dusks' every thrust athrob together
at syrinx split infinities

rained down in daily radiance, no
never did hoedown jamboree
so strum flesh harp

rung out but harbinger of
believe, believe, be Live above!
& bluegrass all about

globe consuming itself, say
brain by spinal Chord
to pierce new universe thrice on

Pulse, thumb plucked upon
time strung celestial circuitry
inset eternal nerve

meddle new bearings,
prescription for sentience—
each cell array galactic vertebrae

Dream: *homestead bound gothic*
grafts archt cherry, plum and peartree
leaved to periphery

Dream: *ask poster hung*
above a bath tiled cobalt blue,
counsels Sage, accepting their prize

"never did eye see sun
unless it had become first sunlike" i.e.
an architecture, music frozen

Mozart to the rafters
intersection many a trail met
as hourglass, wreath/chalice/scepter

or interpret its spaces so as
axis sphinx, on wings
egg center maze, scales midst fountain

a window's light laid sheaf of yellow
lift us threshold zenith,
ever the leveler

ARK 74, ARCHES VIII

(FROM THOREAU'S JOURNALS)

"and something more I saw
left off understanding, around bend
encircling world

Words lie like boulders on a page
woods black as clouds,
blood durable as aqueduct

no surface bare long—
earth covered deep alphabet
this spring laid open with my hoe,

down stream, eyes leveled at you
assume a true sphericity
and bay the moon

multiply deeds within, a cynosure
that every star might fall
into its proper place

being, the great explainer
as if the earth spoke
and heavens crumpled into time

vast glow-worm in fields of ether
as if answered its end,
tail curled about your vitals

sea of mowing, seeing no bottom
leaves ply and flowing fill up path
and thunder near at hand

like summer days seen far away
golden comb, successive lines of haze
set fire to the edges

a crow's wing in every direction,
very deep in the sod
bursting a myriad barrier

as if a cavern unroofed
this great see-saw of brilliants,
oclock strikes whippoorwill

swayed as one, from I know not what
see stars reflected
in the bottom of our boat

chandeliers of darkness
I saw sun shining into like depths,
both planet and the stubble

within compass of a spark
the flute I now hear
on pinnacle, to the end of days

Wing horse, the veery trill
go about search echo
mountains already left these shores

I look under the lids of time,
left without asylum
to gather a new measure

through aisles of ages
art, every stroke of the chisel
enter own flesh and bone

without moving a finger,
turning my very brain
reflected from the grass blades"

ARK 75, ARCHES IX

(FROM VAN GOGH'S LETTERS)

"Picture it! black nets
spread over enormous circles,
white heat of iron

headlong into reality,
turned inside out, upside down
on the road now before me

in the dizzying tangle,
a ditch full of violet irises,
countless buttercup

full quick as lightning
deluge of mind,
entirely absorbed by nature

a spot from which one can see
everything become visible
torched moment,

in a few short strokes
your days numbered,
not destined for the worms

earth—flat—infinite
Horses and men no larger than fleas,
every little speck A Millet

silvery sky above that mud,
to make headway
outside the paint

Imagine then—
The door is wide open
from one night till the other

And that, before I close
my eyes forever,
I shall see the *rayon blanc*

at the back of it all
ardor and fire,
reality too stands gold vertigo

I have rented a house
yellow outside, whitewashed within
in full sun

I shut myself up within myself
like a lighthouse
on an unshakable basis

a terrace with two cypresses,
a nameless black
charged with electricity

Wishing to see a different light,
exile and stranger
I am dead set on my work

we exist neither for one thing
or for the other
but to prepare the way,

chaos in a goblet,
great figures of angels
bread ground between millstones

on that terrible emerald sea
rising up to the very
height of frame"

ARK 76, ARCHES X

riddle iota sublime,
and know no more
than when cast forth garden

a city built caught straws
if clay hold up,
millefleur to the shore

scrutiny, full honeycomb
many thousands feet thru rock
beg quest thereon

towers cliff *ad finitum*
capstone continent,
sea stretch from last species

amongst a summer's rose,
leaf round leaf face inner core
move source target

unto last sheaf reaped
cairn for the dead,
spread many-colored a carpet

magnetic congeries of genes
made up of answers,
meanwhile flinging new question

bareass us barreling nowhere, now
inevitably believable
yet having whale of a time

strung lute, sunset
katydid throng hollyhock
(order too stacked for the odds)

blue horse, yellow shadow
enough throw scarlet off geranium
bloomed windowsill

on path The Secret Garden
equator of blessings
N/E/S/W where Dancer = Carpenter

asleep on Jacob's pillow stone,
flame imprimatur
before oncoming night

where heat sweats wheat,
"for purple mountain majesties
mend every flaw

thoroughfare for more than life,
above the fruited plain
thine alabaster cities gleam

in gold refine thy soul,
crown more than self
impassioned stream beyond the years

for spacious skies shed grace
America! America!
undimmed by freedom sees"

tuningfork unison one violin bow
an arch, in resonance
lept fire to mind in choir

enquire, enquire
bells rise enisled off the deep!
Sat In Great Hymnal Font

ARK 77, ARCHES XI

steeped in makeshift
"one that loved the sun,
and sent its root down deep"

bare record of the word
umbilical, a fellow carpentree
stand but in my head

too much, too soon, fast epitaph
Opus Twin Opposites
helix matter in own right

medallion of spun glass,
sentience itself testament as
ability toll bell

earth spinning its axis
two veins & artery
counterclockwise brain's coil

rib of white whale
to tail pulled blue-eyed lion,
in the middle of nowhere

astride one great divisible,
aurora borealis
thru backward of time

mute, numinous
set to number howmany streaks
on each curl of a tulip

swimming upstream to Messiah
hook line & sinker
arrest in crystal, flow

the wine-dark sea
any Odysseus order as wave,
if snail crawl equal lightspeed

where beast, rare
upon Isle of the Blest reside
shrouded in accuracy

behold stage to stage,
the curtain held
to last pounce intelligence

& revolve about one one's body
almost above notice,
while soul practice nail

any stretch of imagination—
to rise and cry out
like putty in your hands

breezes, Hesperides
feats under great spread wisdome
to speed the day, mold clay

pitchfork the un-sea-sing
and moon stupa sun,
leverage veritable deepenings

actXity sunder brainstem,
storm in the head
countour everything believable

"fraction wave through fraction,
reaction solve reaction"
inVerse salvation

ARK 78, ARCHES XII (THE HYMNALS)

"tell us, Watchman of the night
the raven fire celestial
clear trumpet call

firmament to climb,
Who snare the clouds their way
Shaping a larger liberty

upward still abreast the grave
that turns not back,
manifold the depth beneath

banner streams The lion's mane,
snow-crowned One wreath
in bulwark panoply

Clearer still, and clearer rise
legions Circle round
in regions Past imagining

Of the other side, hosannas
the fence ablaze
an endless Alleluia!

Upwards I fly, beam uncreate
God be in my head
before beat closing eyes

exulting strains
wing my words, that they may
Laud the cup eternity

Till not a stone
was left on stone, lift voice
from tempest: Carpenter

anthem, east to utmost west
Out of The Cloud
Fanfare pole to pole

City not made with hands,
rent asunder
Forth seraph gates

Where light-years frame elect
the Pleiades,
And point Orion's sword

unfathom'd, green Jerusalem
terrestrial ball
built unfurled a Dream

Above the darkling world,
towers Widening sway
the rending tomb

!stones themselves would sing
in comet's train,
interstellar corridors

footsteps sunlit snow at sea
plane, litany, lathe
enraptured main

Peal, in Triune Architect
pure tide confined
pulse antiphon amazing veins

Lead me all my journey through
Wellspring crucified
path open, fountainhead"

ARK 79, ARCHES XIII (THE HYMNALS)

"descend endless realms:
No broader numbered measure
Than man's mind

chariot beyond compare
mid silver shield,
and rolled on wheels of amber

strip I the wind on every side,
clust'ring spheres upheld
far reason's ear

face to face sun
bare ashes, so blind an alley
assembled star by star

O for million pinion tongues,
set apart as cornerstone
over and around us

Where apes swing angels
Three in One, and One in Three
high Skyward wide

words and signs the arches rang
upward still in threshold,
vast order ranged

Rise up Interpreted
crowned flame in borrowed time,
one teeming net of blood

to terminate illusion so,
snow on snow stair steeps of light
dominion mirror clear

sewn radiant hem
who robe a luster within, Ah!
out every corner sing

o'er multitudinous abyss
is, and is to be
dare tell all speech denies

Wrecks endless of storied time,
old world made new
as footsteps ride the wave

ply us, six-winged seraph
Alpha and Omega
cherubim treed sleepless an eye

Kindling anew line lifted of sea,
perfect in messenger
table spread ember hid vow

view fount of life
peal gates of pearl, gates of horn
swimming topaz entwined

all hallowed, ageless amethyst
in the land Of
the glorious Body sing

unseen yet ever near,
sung in unison
stand revealed full man exalt

adorn from chaos' swarm
thirsting beyond bound cIrcle,
soars up Paradise"

ARK 80, ARCHES XIV (THE HYMNALS)

"Gray wakes clad green,
tenement of clay
to put forth matchless rose

seed Marvels all sung globe
harp hung crimson bough
Inspired epiphany,

beat sword plowshare
bed spear, To pruning hook
snatch diamond teeming mire

Till rise and set no more
unmoved, all motion's source
scan livelong night

Finger put whirlwind
consumed on high, wing words
they seas might wrestle

rapt in vision, fiery pillar
Name all names above
a rock on which to build

void bottom, brim or shore
image swan darkness
Driven from wondrous frame

mansion beyond swelling flood
anthem sparkling raiment
evermore, Magnificat

Water break forth starlight
a crystal pavement,
brightness bowed as stone

from each opening vein
to lift our eyes
inmost page apostle, prophet

assembled essence
to let the world go by
watchfires knocking the door

Beyond the dark and narrow,
chart and compass
the bright immensities

breadth 'yond perpetual length
Dove, Consummation
never ebbing Pentecost

all our aim ends
of one piece, and woven
lamp hasten old blossom center

clap hands, clap hands
to remotest golden sands awake
in Cradled prize

unseen yet ever near
Quickened elect,
ripened transcending partaker

shrined within,
thirst countless number
though round destruction walk

strike, host to host complete
snow-crowned hosannas
forward into light"

ARK 81, ARCHES XV

Noah on board
(Dialogue between Eddy & Flo)
agenda: eternal purr

aardvark to zebu, two by two
dove proffer olive twig
—intuit summit

come plain to inhabit
bedrock America,
speech stretched unto Babel

one in many, ring in a pool
(thought bytheby
hitherto impossible)

eternal triangle,
Present fulcrum Past Future
scythe through harvest

gods come to earth here,
warp shuttle woof
white robes like fluted cloud

World Pole, blue ladder
with dandelion whelm old lawn
pinwheel at the top

Emerson, pilot County Clipper
"give me the eye to see
a navy in an acorn"

(out of almost nowhere,
a leaping school bold dolphins
appears alongside)

first dance! then choreograph
Brain teamed Sperm
partition fired partition

astride, as burningglass
full face company
"& plant there trees in three"

where preacher bird
perch loftest branch, to hail
far come red burly suns

voluntary, irrevocable
born of ocean to puncture sky
and die pled blood

synthesis surpassing synthesis,
ride whatever whirlwind
"splinter very orb"

sun on the rigging
bound beyond Cape of Good Hope,
upon the good ship *Praxis*

ivy wrapped round thyrsus
consensus: scatter
bright spear twined wheatsheaf

feather, sun, and Holy Ghost
to state it! man alone
exfoliate felicities

spun roots strike flint,
arbor vitae come full circle
even six feet under

ARK 82, ARCHES XVI

ride gained ring of fire
erase, reinforce
red came the rain down that day

shot right to heart of rumor,
bush burning inner bush
gather new measure

electric with infinities sped
steel, salt spray
La Tour Eiffel in effect

primeval survival
sharpshooting Chartres
fed the old, eternal furnace

by dawn's early marigold
attend always zenith,
contained of spark a compass

every stroke of the chisel, air
in speaking distance
enter own flesh and bone

you see whose pews are whose
a deity *en plein aire*,
grace laid rest

thus Chopin: "continuous
and even as a hair"
thistle inside out upsidedown

all years it takes,
code splice forth astonishment
bowed gut the only speech

exfoliate unfailingly
rhyme as mortar,
always a little dizzy each step

giddyap then here and now
any-when or -where
—the rest may be Jerusalem—

mane of wind as Adam of clay
logos, thunder of hooves
flat out the land

earthwhirl, *Cirque*
de Soleil striped blue/white
on rockinghorse universe

any rag-tag and bobtail,
your name written all over it!
absolute brouhaha

wherein hierarchies of speed
stagger the senses,
stones astonished light

decked boondocks
—slight flint flight sheath
surround us, evangelick

experience all plowed in
arrowhead of flame,
makes room lucid heaven's root

as a wind streak empty prairie
capstone to spire
steed, aleap tumbleweed

ARK 83, ARCHES XVII, THE RAMP

FOR GLENN TODD

A siege of herons and bitterns
an herd of swans,
of cranes, and of curlews

a dopping of sheldrakes, a
spring of teals
covert of coots, gaggle of geese

a pedelyng of ducks, a skein of
geese, muster of
peacocks, bevy of quails

a congregation of plovers or
covey of partridges, a
flight of doves

a cast of hawks, a wisp
of snipes, a fall of woodcocks
a brood of hens

a building of rooks
a murmuration of starlings, an
exaltation of larks

a flight of swallows, host of
sparrows, watch of
nightingales, charm of goldfinches

a pride of lions
a leap of leopards, an herd of
harts, of buck and deer

bevy of roes, a sloth of bears
a singular of boars
a sounder of wild swine

a route of wolves, a harrass
of horses, rag of colts
a stud of mares

a pace of asses, barren of
mules, oxen team
a drove of kine, flock of sheep

a tribe of goats
a sculk of foxes, a sett
of badgers, riches of martens

a ponder of elephants, a husk
or down of hares, and
of rabbits a nest

clowder of cats, a shrewdness
of apes, labour of moles
all in the same boat

"You shall say a hart
harboureth, a buck lodgeth
a roe beddeth

A hare seateth or formeth
a coney sitteth,
and a fox is uncased

Dislodge a buck
start a hare, unkennel a fox
rowse hart, bowlt coney

Hart belloweth, roe belleth
hare beateth, fox
barketh, wolf howleth"

ARK 84, ARCHES XVIII

so roareth handprint Lion
"there sits fire
with the forest in his mouth"

so spouteth whale
no letup or brook back,
on long unconscionable musics

Down to the wire, strum plenitude
stranger from birth
Occur. Transpire. Effect.

artifact, from artifact
Perfect of Kind
pryed out ardor increase order

double to that which is,
bringeth shadow death to light
secure as morning

surrounded by splinters of fire
all covered with flesh—
earth winged in sun

catwhisker-met universe
one skiey bailiwick
like unto palpable Empyrean,

handlettered bandshell
both Leviathan, Behemoth sport
amid too few days

claim of the vast
that real article/particle
sometimes seen as One

like eyelids of the dawn,
yawneth crocodile
to coax anew the sun

meadowlark afoot,
wide the leafworld roll forth
who knocketh fiery door

Among dross, treasure
out through far back of night
from star to star

Comes then Conqueror Worm,
come bones of earth
come throes of change upon us

summon the vale of flesh
through granite vein, call up
again first gaze

comes giant tread of Sphinx
comes whirling axe,
dark hand emerge Abyss

scales so near another
no air could slip their weave,
maketh path to shine

hast thou clothed his neck
with thunder
who swalloweth ground?

answered whirlwind:
he taketh it between his eyes,
not upon earth his like

ARK 85, ARCHES XIX

Craft, to seek renewal

askew all question

& exit in resonance genesis

passion for truth,

mutual ritual channel energies

to forge again moon sun

Velocity, giver of forms

actual vehicle

through higher tighter a fire

passage exeunt Blake Gate,

echoes of the first story shrine

faith in experience

Accord fertility

most immediate a source,

still point of turning world

empty, and of an air
extraordinarily swift and clear
—cataract into crucible

bear witness,
who live out their dream
down to the ground

beheld above the sky
skull rampart,
sprout aburning bushes new

unconquerable paradigm
bear witness, all too mortal
tiger by the tail

happenstance, pulled in dance
tumbleweed electric
o'er everyday a prairie

sonar of reason
interlave whale plunge Whole,
become illumed periphery

leap hoop utter unknown,
pearled cloud hurtling within
both rim and door

bear witness influx choir
in "thousand celestial ardours,
where he stood"

elan, spread noontide
elm-filled night
magnificent of insignificance

as home is you being yourself,
hearsay state sane line
to greet the day

Talisman, alert
"directed at the nameless
innermost & incessant" choice

whistling down the wind
husband a land,
self bound furrowed horizon

bluer as hill rise above hill
apportioned lot, behave
who Art in heaven

ARK 86, ARCHES XX, THE WREATH

wreathe sagebrush lilac
heart's ease, celandine entwine
trillium chrysanthemum

larkspur tigerlily
nonesuch mother-of-thousands,
rocket with tansy twirl

honeysuckle coil heliotrope
wistaria, anemone
cockscomb within clematis

weld phlox amaranth
saxifrage asplit the rock
to eyebright, aster and galax

jewelweed jump-up Jacob's ladder
andromeda, daffodil field
trefoil angelica

holly, yet hyacinth weave
clover o'er arrowhead
jack-in-the-pulpit tumbleweed

ivy twist up sunflower,
daisy whirl iris compassplant
snakeroot hellebore

bindweed into waterlily
spin ranunculus,
pearly-everlasting eglantine

lavender broider violet
braid foxglove fleur-de-lis
azalea, bergamot

speedwell balm dogwood
rosemary memory,
burning bush/touch-me-not

gentian ply geranium,
ply thistle to Solomon's seal
orchis whistle-up calamus

of crowsfoot, dandelion
of firethorn peony periwinkle
construct a wreath

plait laurel with poppy
sumac, pitcherplant
tulip penstemon trumpetflower

candlewick maidenhair
bittersweet acanthus, nonesuch
plait milfoil life-of-man

bird's eye blazing star
rose goldenrod
ladder-to-heaven, Joseph's coat

lily of the valley
briar bird-of-paradise,
zinnia any stonecrop alyssum

skyrocket steeple-bush
lion's mouth, scarlet lightning
upstart wormwood

bloodroot twined red hot poker
nightshade, asphodel
all gathered in a garland

ARK 87, ARCHES XXI

and bid yr ghosts to revel
here and now with us
again, yet feast

as gave blood to shades
Odysseus, gone down sea again
up out of Erebos

swarming from every direction
hordes of the dead,
under earth of wide way

every insect a-hum
of imagination, figment
though summon up grass itself

say, ransack psyche
ouster of shadow a Host
Camera Obscura

errand to speak a truth
Shaker of Earth,
Helios who sees all things

gravid with *lux*
put spine to feathers
far, the rafters and back

over the banister reeling
touch match to pyre
you're it! Amok Deus

Starboard, framed boat
step ashore different world
multicolor of wheel

shroud shrug shroud
as glass vessel cloud over,
soul moveth the waters

spirit crowd ahead, upheld
vaporized harpsichord
torrent on hot surface

(O lost in adulation
no, never anon
commit one memory to flame)

impact planetesimals
ripe for gravity
drawn to face of the planet

fireball flung cold depths
of space, bombard
molt crust from within

come to surface
covered broad blue oceans,
chain of extinction

hit meteorite spermoi
tulip of flame
galvanized, gulping oxygens

sun blanket rock floor,
put up great building blocks
acrown our path

all things writ here
incident crater simulacrum
—enact last day

ARK 88, ARCHES XXII

cue: the end of a thing,
signal for another
as clue unroll ball of thread

cosmos sprung puissant
snail's pace primordial soup,
march on horizon

down maze of shade shaft sun
open any a door—
and all is technicolor

without lifting a finger
inhabitant Hinterland
transmission, instantaneous

through aisles withstood ages,
cirrus-winged horses
just lighted on the earth

fled jonquil many a dawn
all sky above alive with larks,
immemorial parliament

down through thunderclaps
and vortex night,
a-molecular curlicues

incandescent coruscation
pillars of fire
on plinth flesh, named hymn

posture outright,
and every torrent sonorous
contagion evangelical

without asylum left, path
lift us up to zenith
at length become fixed stars

replica of the upper room
(the lower as yet unfinished)
charisma, Chimaera

register canticles,
every atom once within a sun
sailing on reflected sky

lilies, immaculate of field
I have considered
and yon tigers thereof

Collect lights as possible,
slice day to see
broad range spun night

from rock, life crammed
gateway any-pulled sea shore O
hell bent for space

still footprint souls
diadem split within tablet,
centuries afield

Suspect the core
Suspend laid law
Surprise the end

cart me out, Ye galaxy
each eye affixed turret
flying the marble kite

ARK 89, ARCHES XXIII, THE CAVE

up from the bones of earth,
hew plasma stone
eye lent by granite

middle of a lake
scroll on malachite scroll
topaz city, Samarkand

downdrift X'd celadon,
chalcedony zephyr
sapphires surpassing rapture

Perfect in detail,
one opalized reptile skeleton
(found Australia 1909)

One snowball geode
lined within pyrite phantoms,
in shape of the earth

One bloodstone panorama
whole starred sky,
beasts portrayed in porphyry

luminous and ominous
open cupboard of chrysoprase,
set lapis-lazuli as Seas

Beneath the surface
root hexagonal crystals
upward, many multiples a water

seams aflame in luster
—Mind amid a play of colors
banded impurities

cut readily in all directions
taking high polish,
universal building stone

an Age of Bronze,
ores of peacock copper
tarnished with iridescence

Mercury wrung cinnabar
rooms prism rooms
pillars of basalt, obsidian

quartzlight, mother-of-pearl
cluster bristling embryo
self caught in amber

heavens gem Clay
layered, full play of time
days onyxed with night

Stir moment alabaster!
Pour cup silvery
Step chance by needle ends

memorable pebbles
rolled mountain torrent,
arrested prime amethyst falls

emerald, revealer-of-truth
noinnerfirehid ruby
fit for a King's finger

hands mirror diamond maker
Adam, engoldened
enter into the Grotto

ARK 90, ARCHES XXIV

meteor lay floor Concordance
here death shall have
narrow dominion

flood mirror ahead
(Immanence trebling within)
lilac, fireflies' abode

free'll buy you nowhere
"a Florida adorable"
if you don't shoulder bounds

sunrise youth's imaginings
road out of the plain,
bicycle yr Ozs

The Great Gaze Bonfire!
aspirant no thread Ariadne's,
yet pant for breath

refraction light of surface
aleap rare Deeps,
antler locked antler

or gazelles of faculties
sprung to mind, full catapult
hit after direct hit

carried in language of music
—great tangible images
to pasture far Mars

algebra the farbetween
and neverbefore,
bore through canopy of time

rock basis of space,
winged chariot hurrying near
to forge ahead New World

just rim the edge of it
wind wave & stars
Life: re-electable cohesion

bloodstream backtobeginning
forest of thorns,
so knock the Messenger

our eye on a universe
set in the eye of a raven,
Master of Revels

ring up dawn upon dawn
and bring suns down,
The Greatest Show on Earth

yes, magic carpet
made up of propeller runways
and helicopter inroads

falls-leaper, water-walker
thoughts held the race
in Wizard blazonry

held like a Banner,
dixieyankeedoodle sparkler
shining ever a distance

if Gods there be to address,
read out *scrapture*
released planet's snare

MEMORIAL DAY, 1990

ARK 91, ARCHES XXV

Off top of my head
seed, honeycomb, vine curl,
shells, snake on branch

mind in orderly array—
forms molded trial & error
living out suitcase

the tide and toll of time
plus pull of space,
snowstorms by starlight

a landscape of Simulars,
where shape sort inked shape
old as the hills

lept dolphin-wise,
plow many psyched that sea
absolutely unbottomed

balance the raftered known
so knock The Messenger,
a door open on

so steady a prestidigitation,
any scene summoned
swirled forth first core

each one faster than the last,
angels upon ladders
vanish Archimboldo elms

wild card shot human deck:
Maypole of image
& compass indissoluble

to oar the Uproar!
yet cross to bear, row to hoe
hollering down town well

knock in the dark
the key to the horizon, yours—
don't lock up behind

yet only by secret handshake
under the Mallorn trees,
and get out fast

(a roll far thunder)
furrow albeit ready ground—
Seasons taken for a ride

gallop, wrapped the world
bold Aurora Borealis
all in an opening of a drawer

"these trees will be my books"
over my dead leaves . . .
hide how we can

face of the deep,
stars through unmeasured
heights of pendant atmosphere

only winged imagination
cement horsesense,
no fall of an apple unforeseen

Unfolding worlds before us,
atom become unto flesh
branched pitchfork

ARK 92, ARCHES XXVI

up from springs of earth
Windmill many exists, armlift
fanned single flame

revenant, lost hearth
anoint renewal
Host of Makeshift, Inn of Sand

one sniff of the Rose,
one step beyond timberline,
in snare of stars

(taking off, in quiet bustle
angels small as moths
assemble Saturn)

scaffold, Mappemonde
a door open upon
gold bees now cymbal struck

on lovely a roll
worlds in a drop of water,
Eden hid an eyeblink

as curled wood forth plane
announce carpenter,
won intricate vernacular

wrestling the abstract
incised on dreams, mankind
barbwire identity

"from morning to bed
I go resounding with music"
—complete astonishment

Sphinx, tricks up sleeves,
one perfect day
comes trial beyond fire

wolf at door, vultures pounce
bears in our cupboard,
mice under floors

"I walked the other evening
to the end of earth,
touched sky with finger"

shook foundations belief
vis-à-vis de rien
gaze tunneled inward,

eagle burst through window
hurtling cottage
a panic of darkness

Then when Mahler dropped
exhausted on a sofa,
a crow flew out from under it

dread apparition
... so knock The Messenger
haven, one battlefield

strummer beyond
The Sunflowers stand aside,
mirrors turn to wall

goals into bloom
in conscious, inexhaustible
corner asylum garden

ARK 93, ARCHES XXVII

FOR JESS

blown dandelion, soapbubble
beyond the pale
"miraculous eclipse"

to draw attention
—tapestry of enchantments
another Think coming

specific, yet metaphorical
jigsaw in overall flux
integral to Realm

hive, radioactive
The Garden of Forking Paths
pasteup switch pasteup

emblematic and magical,
Look into the glass
pattern upon opposed pattern

converging & diverging heart
heroic Narkissos!
1,000 figures on a swing

versions = visions
(adjacent heraldic phenomena)
eyes under earth's lid

reborn throughout range,
Orpheus in asphodel
bonds electric hide-and-seek

universe as mirror dimension
—what might not happen?
gathering Alchemies

Soul carry us on
impassioned, waking destiny
follow childhood's ball

dissolved slant happenstance
at play, emblazoned
full populace unbound!

a community epic, cyclical
hung in the balance
stream sweet Time

Vanish ravine, Reveal peak
barbed perimeter
shapes throng a span

thunderous incharged cloud
"about to wake up"
mercurial, inescapable

rapture and beyond
pass by, The Prince of Araby
figured out held flame

flesh asudden possessed
arm in arm the swarm
shoot the works, "Ifs" embraced

carried panoply circumstance
disjunct abundance,
zones Imaginations fill

appear "great blossomer"
stars reflected minute pools
Seraphic multitude

ARK 94, ARCHES XXVIII

Inhabitant fireline
each step a leap in the dark
—earth buckle underfoot

new landscape explore
i.e., a + b = etc.
down to finched square mile

blue cliff waterfall,
thrushcall encompass vastness
Rose x Skyline

grainfield with grasshoppers
led Nextdoor Nowhere,
swept away in avalanche

Snowflake, own stronghold
equatorial upheaval
(so poles gather new measure)

as starry asylum
cypress lined blurred lamp
temple on the edge blank plain

unlearn passage of night
unlearn sight's maze,
insist pavement astronomical

nether mown galaxy,
every leaf catching the sun
(look at looking at it)

peel far end of the sky
inch paws darkling,
phalanx Excelsior illustrious

how stone encandled rose,
how agate-edged unto Aldebaran
ultimately triumphant

gaze, whorled rule of thumb
led brush Cezanne
surge long toil of grace

What will I tell in it?
but jolt amazements of being
wholly imagination

in logic of a dream,
as Klieg-light shafts cloud
hierarchies of Most Real

enlist radiant continuum
whose name is Legion
vault home, we've no choice

multimelodious at combustion!
of dandelion aperture
heel struck crystalline ray

headlands, Ultima Thule
compass swing ablaze horizon
cell trigger cell

torn limb from limb,
tightrope unscaled heights
appear before your Lord

thrust kindle counterthrust,
matrix pale infinity
garden, before The Fall

ARK 95, ARCHES XXIX

FOR STAN BRAKHAGE

access, accelerated day
make Foundry ring
delight! delight! delight!

doubt reduced to dust
Nobody but demand windfall,
due heights within

arcade cadence arcade
fabric, one fluted blaze
nested set of cycles respond

sounding sword, Heaven's edge
full sight unsealed
dazzle snowball in Hell

no bounds but belief
Gods, who walk the world
crosses intercross in a cloud

thistledown drawing chariot
mirrored furnace of old,
doomed Pandemonium

Old feedback bravado
light, pulling all directions
wound inkling down abyss

(filmed sea unveil sky
up to chest, camera in hand
Paradise *sans* lens)

(winds whistling off prairie,
anointed leveler
pyramid split infinities)

whirled round ahead
cast forth eternal garden
by hand, electric, of the Lord

banked with flowers, candles
System (solar) discus
as flies buzz rosebud bush

or dread hounds nose
heart, any springboard escape
body sundered by stars

soul's last sheaf reaped
engoldened cairn,
Maelstrom itself prolonged

riddled into gospel,
in the Middle of Outhere
locusts descending summer skies

the whole dealt galaxy
Asparkling flood of worlds,
treed silhouette

all tempered speed & distance,
Damask in/out about
great wings of blackbird

set down the Isle of Man
—raindrop poised single leaf—
wide crystal ball

wonders within radius, a
dreamed Hesperides
rare realms saved endlessly

ARK 96, ARCHES XXX

"The silver light
turned every blade of grass,
every particle of sand

into a luminous
metallic splendor, there was
nothing however small

that did not clash
in the bright wind, that
did not send

arrows of light
through the glassy air"
wrote Ansel Adams!

All night, at golden hive
busiest of Being
lustrous intelligence

cast throughout darkness,
tackling the eternal
bluest guitar

set against Time
roll back yr mortal lids,
sentry of statuary

innumerable numinosities
mind set ajar,
thru wildering gyre

throat aloft, afloat—
truths to the World's edge
grace amazing tell

outside the door
red wheelbarrow glint rain,
Anyone might see it

let up the blinds
as sap mount into tree,
scribed lark in jubilation

magnetic, torch antiphony
tail universe end/on
waltz seasons all four

death sweet be not yet,
I tread the stars
in perilous anatomy

over bottomless pit
only intricater,
I thread evolving Heaven

"nequaquam vacuum"
flamestich I symmetries:
weaver oriole's nest

I construct ahive
suns one can't gaze upon
surpassing foresight,

only Hand with Language
nothing unknowable
fate, the Undoer

home everlasting
(memory, tenacious anemone)
await composer Sword

ARK 97, ARCHES XXXI

Hero, arrow true
(knock hallowed messenger
how fashion destiny)

inherit chaos without a lid,
the world made flesh
"Sermon of the Inanimate"

held fast in enchantment
Eureka! sparkled ferris wheel
inexhaustible herald

harmonies, harmonies
breath to follow thread
Shadow safe through labyrinth

further and further under
harvest of shades,
hanged by very thumbs

Doubt myth of orchard
Shape new wholes
Alone, kindle known world

angels bright-winged
bear up the Host,
humdrum how rush of being

athroat, thought multiplied
inchoate *Son & Lumière*
rapt burning bush

hand over hand in path
imperishable, blaze of self
threshold Pantheon

Soul shook bounds,
the invisible made manifest
catharsis every corner

breeched bellies of Whales
realm within realm,
forth on a terrible sea

nor will Nought triumph
unhorsed before firmament
wishes: phenomena

as if before flourish
innate hush of Holy Ghost
—galactic nightingales

a breath interrupt molecule:
scythe sunflower thicket
archive anonymous

swift the years offer
ever more difficult births
lightning, a diadem

a shape-gathered darkness
anchor of years,
furnace behind the sky

hawk, heavenward
hierarchy hurdle hierarchy
if world enough & time

quintessence in chorus
sapphire Hemisphere
deeps, crowned with stars

ARK 98, ARCHES XXXII

Deluge needle's eye
swimming rarest ethers
a lexicon seek, ineluctable

each peak a torrent
each span a spinning parterre,
deep pit open each step

erased for sure, shores
in split-second transformation
a cornfield (Kansas)

dead set against order,
tempest past tense,
Unknown smashed smithereens

when all the winds are loosed
four corner, cloven flame
The New Jerusalem

in paean to the elements
uproot Apocalypse,
wheel within burnished wheel

swallowed by great Leviathan
then eyes, awakening
trumpets out every crack

few minutes left,
Lord set me on fire to say
persistence primeval

now and now forever
is all we know of Deity,
undoubted beauty

& ear to Orpheus' seashell
far shelters beatitude,
upheld decorum

frome byss to abyss
all elements transfigured,
give voice to prophecy

winged brow & feet of clay,
anew dimensions
cast forth plumed Death

in terrors of energy, elect
sing Body Electric
who trailblaze the mind

—only one small boy survive
to discover universe
an aerie forever

then hold galaxies
up 4th of July sparkler
hid, O hid in the lilac bush

Manifestations: red sun
once in a blue moon,
yellow dandelions on mown lawn

great organ tones
out center of the earth
and hills escape their bound,

wave crash upon wave:
cycle uproot cycle Hereafter
thunder wine-dark horizon

ARK 99, ARCHES XXXIII

Aship, reel in fountainhead
enclosure of roses
skies indigo, gold moon

Omphalos triumphant
"only connect"
end, point of beginning

of old, apotheosis
chandelier *fond du lac*
cross (mortal) hid boundary

compass beyond confines
music of the spheres solved,
mosaic of Cosmos

snowflakes lit darkest sea,
bowsprit the deeps
bound white antipodes

such conflagration of souls
Dawn in Erewhon,
corporeal cornucopia

one being surround in bloom
flow essential seed
portal system Milky Way

as Unmoved Mover under orders
axis mundi, ascend scale
organism omnipotent

poised in flesh,
awake horns psaltery
Fanfare for the Common Man

mind set razor an edge,
blood fulfill final ablution
fire purify baton

Oompapah! to lead the band
any stray orchestra
knows who destination

core of the universe
(so rings redwood of eons)
gospel sentience

Lo! *allegro non troppo*
remake mankind,
a joyous noise into the void

"from going to and fro
in the earth, and from walking
up and down in it"

as speech arc Simulacrum, O
chorus us Homo Sapiens
in a major key!

tools, consonant & vowel
to fashion a voice
commensurate wheel of time

Origins great aorta
leaved from the wrist up, but
yet to attain the skies

all arrowed a rainbow midair,
ad astra per aspera
countdown for Lift Off

AFTERWORD / ABOUT THE AUTHOR

AFTERWORD

To spend twenty-odd years writing a poem, undeterred by risks and ship-wrecks of those before, would seem sheer folly. They stand before me, great obstacles. Ezra Pound, only a long afternoon in Venice, waving farewell with his cane, in sparkling background the canal he associated with the writing of *A Lume Spento* . . . William Carlos Williams, maybe a half-dozen visits to Rutherford when I was a student at Columbia, rife with sparky theory for American vernacular . . . More closely, Louis Zukof-sky and Charles Olson, braving new schemes for language—The Mini-malist and The Maximus—such opposing poles of influence: parities.

But I knew I'd my own tack to take. If my confreres wanted to write a work with all history in its maw, I wished, from the beginning, to start all over again, attempting to know nothing but a will to create, and matter at hand. William Blake would be a guiding spirit: his advice to pay at-tention every moment: the very lightning, then thunder: a voice out of a cloud.

A turning point was a visit to Le Facteur Cheval's *Le Palais Ideal* in Hautrives, France. Cheval claimed that on his postman's rounds he kicked a stone one day, then suddenly conceived the idea of building a palace "like a dream." In one moment of vision he was Everyman who attempts creative quest. Later, Simon Rodia's Watts Towers, raising a new realm of mosaic from a Los Angeles slum, gave me a new armature of possibilities.

The idea of *ARK* came when I was able at last to conceive it a structure rather than diatribe, artifact rather than argument, a veritable shell of the chambered nautilus, sliced and polished, bound for Ararat unknown. Of stout pioneer stock, grandson of prairie settlers come to Kansas in a covered wagon, I grew up in no concert with ideas whatsoever, on land devoid of communal landmark, smack in the middle of windy flat expanse of grass. Over such reaching gulf, who could resist constructing an Ozymandias of the spirit?

I wrote in an early note to *The Foundations*: "Let us imagine inside these covers a monument dedicated *Bison bison bison* (imagine it so carved) at base, and located if place could be put, on those shelving prairies between Ashland and Dodge City, Kansas, as a span between Big and Little Basins, centering over St. Jacob's Well. This near-legendary 'bottomless' pool can be looked up in *National Geographic*, but as I knew it in childhood it was a real magic place tales were told of as exciting as those from the Brothers Grimm." As Gertrude Stein said, "anyone is as their land and air is."

An architecture, *ARK* is fitted together with shards of language, in a kind of cement of music. Based on trinities, its cornerstones the eye, the ear, the mind, its three books consist of *The Foundations*, of which there are thirty-three beams, *The Spires*, of which there are thirty-three built on top, with thirty-three arcades of *The Ramparts* rounding the periphery. The first book goes from sunrise to noon, the second ends at sunset with only Mt. Ossa set on Pelion reflecting back light. The third is a night of the soul. My central myth is that of Orpheus and Euridice, the blessed argument between poet and muse, man and his anima. Orpheus, who made the trees bend and animals one with his lyre. Orpheus, the beheaded voice floating downstream.

To the left of the entrance of his *Palais Ideal*, Cheval erected a special niche for tools he'd spent near a lifetime wielding. It is one of art's most eloquent signatures. A sturdy desk, adjustable lamp, and typewriter is all any poet can claim for tools. On either side Cheval placed giants. For me these would take the form of Zukofsky's poetry (via Mallarmé) along with the prose of Edward Dahlberg, a mentor of Olson. From them I learned music and concision.

Also, certainly Charles Ives, who wove patriotic anthem and church hymn into his work, like breathing, was a major influence. The texts I pulled into the fabric of *ARK* usually identify themselves as such—as in the Hymnal "Ramparts" which are constructed from words and phrases of Protestant hymns. To be found is a scrambled "Battle Hymn of the Republic" and "America the Beautiful," which anyone should be able to pick out.

However, a couple do not announce themselves except in poem titles. "Palms" (in section 21, 22, and 23) is made from the Psalms, word after word in sequence. Section 47, my quarrel with my hometown, Ashland, includes a "real" volcano spewing ash topped by "The Majesnehry" (Henry James), which reads his Niagara Falls backward to achieve a jet over it all.

RONALD JOHNSON / SAN FRANCISCO, 1991

ABOUT THE AUTHOR

Ronald Johnson was born on November 25, 1935 in Ashland, Kansas, a small town on the prairie about twenty miles north of the Oklahoma border. This is frontier land, where Midwestern agriculture meets the Western range. Ashland is situated in the heart of legendary cowboys and Indians territory: Dodge City and Medicine Lodge are both nearby. Red gypsum hills and windswept expanses mark the landscape; bracing winter winds, springtime lilacs, and summertime sand-hill plums mark the seasons. It was here that Johnson spent the first eighteen years of his life.

Johnson enrolled at the University of Kansas, where he stayed a year before he was drafted into the army. This was 1954, a year after the conclusion to the Korean War. He spent the entire two years of his service in the United States, stationed at various army bases, earning money for college through the G.I. Bill. In 1958, preparing to enter Columbia University, he met Jonathan Williams on a visit to Washington, D.C. The two quickly entered a romantic partnership that lasted a decade, taking up residence together in New York. Johnson involved himself in his studies, and the two spent their free time with members of the Black Mountain College community who had migrated to New York after the closure of that experimental school (which Williams had attended). Thanks in part to Williams's ongoing publishing activities with the Jargon Society, their contacts included Charles Olson, William Carlos Williams, Louis Zukofsky, as well as numerous other poets who would become associated with the emerging "New American Poetry." These constituted Johnson's education in poetry: his degree from Columbia and his immersion in the world of mid-century experimental writing. In 1964, the Jargon Society issued Johnson's first book, *A Line of Poetry, a Row of Trees*.

With Jonathan Williams as his mentor and guide, Johnson undertook two significant journeys in the early sixties: he walked the length of the Appalachian Trail, from New York to Georgia, and he spent the greater part of two years wandering around England (with later excursions to Europe). Both of these journeys informed his work, especially in the value he placed on direct observation and his sense of company as central to literature. In England, Johnson paid homage to Basil Bunting and made friends with Ian Hamilton Finlay, both enduring influences. In 1967, Johnson saw published his second book of poetry, *The Book of the Green Man*, a seasonal poem about the autochthonous, verdurous mythical figure of the title; at the same time, he was actively publishing concrete poetry with Doyle Moore's Finial Press in Urbana, Illinois.

In 1969, Johnson and Williams parted ways when Johnson settled in San Francisco, where he would remain for over twenty-five years. During this time he published several volumes of poetry, including *Valley of the Many-Colored Grasses* in 1969, *Songs of the Earth* in 1970, and *Radi os* in 1977. The latter is a rewriting-by-excision of Milton's *Paradise Lost* and one of the first erasure poems. To support himself, Johnson held many jobs: he worked as a cook, a caterer, a manager of a bar and of a restaurant; as a clerk in a gift shop; occasionally as a visiting poet at a university; but mostly, he earned money writing cookbooks. The best known of these is *The American Table*, which assembles recipes of American regional cooking replete with anecdotes from Johnson's travels among poets and others. Johnson called it "the diet of the tribe." During these years, he lived in an apartment at 73 Elgin Park, below Market Street and just above the Mission District, keeping costs down by taking on a roommate. During the days, he tested out recipes for the cookbooks. In the evenings, he wrote poetry, corresponded with other writers, and read science-fiction novels. Part of his social reality was defined by his role as a founder and road captain of the Rainbow Motorcycle Club, a gay social club described by Johnson as a "band of lusty roistering men, often partying till dawn." Out of this routine, *ARK* was constructed.

Johnson began *ARK* in 1970, when (as described in "BEAM 2") he was thirty-five years old, midway through his life, according to the Dantean formula. Initially, he called the poem "Wor(l)ds," a working title that persisted almost until the publication of *ARK: The Foundations* in 1980. Composing the poem serially, in the model of the American modernist long poem, he continued to work on it for over twenty years. He completed the final section on New Year's Eve, 1990.

In the early 1990s, health and financial problems sent Johnson back to Kansas, to Topeka, to live with his father (his mother had passed away years before). A brain tumor was discovered and removed, but he never fully recovered. Around this time, he began working at Ward-Meade Historic Park, where he served as a handyman, baker, and gardener. He claimed the job kept him in money for "scotch, cigarettes, and cat food." Because he was a veteran, the government provided for his healthcare.

His needs were few; he continued to live with his father in various houses in Topeka. In 1996, a complete edition of *ARK* appeared from Living Batch Press.

While working at Ward-Meade, Johnson began to compose the work that would be his last, published posthumously as *The Shrubberies*: these were poems of observation, compression, and subtle music. Many were drawn from the sights and sounds of the extensive gardens at Ward-Meade. Meanwhile, his health continued to worsen. In 1997, he succumbed to a stroke that left him debilitated, the result of new brain tumors. He died on March 4, 1998.